Level 2 Award for Personal Licence Holders (APLH) Licensing Manual

2018 Edition

Corinne Tuplin
LLB Law (Hons) Solicitor

Copyright © Pro-Leagle Publishing 2009-2018
All rights reserved.

This print edition is published in the United Kingdom by Pro-Leagle Publishing, an imprint of Pro-Leagle Wired, via CreateSpace, an Amazon company: Amazon UK Services Ltd, 60 Holborn Viaduct, London EC1A 2FD, United Kingdom.

Please direct sales or editorial enquiries to: support@proleaglewired.com
www.proleaglewired.com

No part of this book may be reproduced or transmitted in any form or by any means electronic or mechanical including photocopying, recording, or by any information storage and retrieval system unless such content is expressly referenced as being licensed from a third party under a license which permits such reproduction or transmission, or unless permission is sought and granted in writing from the copyright holder.

Selected images used in this publication have been released into the public domain by their authors and may be reused accordingly at the discretion of those authors. This does not provide the right to reuse any original Pro-Leagle Publishing photography. To confirm copyright status of images you wish to reuse please contact the copyright holder.

The terms and conditions of usage of the Level 2 APLH Licensing Manual and the contents of this book shall be governed and interpreted in accordance with the laws of England and Wales.

Pro-Leagle Publishing and the author make every effort to ensure that the material and information contained in this manual is as accurate as possible. However, we give no warranty of any kind regarding this manual and/or materials therein provided. Neither Pro-Leagle Publishing nor the author make any representations or warranties of any kind (express or implied) as to the accuracy, completeness, currency, or reliability of any of the content or data found in the manual.

To the fullest extent as permitted by law Pro-Leagle Publishing and the author expressly exclude all liability whatsoever for any loss or damage howsoever arising out of the use of this manual or reliance upon the content of the same. In no event shall Pro-Leagle Publishing or the author be liable for any damages, losses, injuries or claims or any direct, indirect, incidental, consequential damages of any kind (including but not limited to lost profits, data or savings) howsoever arising (including, but not limited to, as a result of Pro-Leagle Publishing's or the author's negligence) in connection with the use of this manual; or any failure or delay of the use or inability to use any component of this manual.

ISBN-10: 1495352196
ISBN-13: 978-1495352195

Contents

1. Overview of the Level 2 APLH Licensing Manual 9
2. Introduction 13
   2.1. The Licensing Act - the New Regime 13
3. Licensable Activities 17
   3.1. The Sale By Retail of Alcohol 18
   3.2. When Will You be Exempt from Requiring a Licence to Sell Alcohol? - The Seven Exemptions 19
   3.3. The Supply of Alcohol on Behalf of a Club to a Club Member 21
   3.4. Provision of Late Night Refreshment 22
   3.5. The Provision of Regulated Entertainment 22
   3.6. Unauthorised Licensable Activities 26
   3.7. Licensable Activities Review Questions 28
4. Alcohol in a Nutshell 31
   4.1. Alcoholic Strength and 'ABV' 32
   4.2. How do you Calculate Units of Alcohol? 32
   4.3. Labelling Laws for Alcoholic Drinks - Clear Labelling of Strength (ABV) Required 33
   4.4. Physiological Effects of Alcohol 34
   4.5. Sensible Drinking and Health Benefits 37
   4.6. Alcohol in a Nutshell Review Questions 39
5. Licensing Authorities 41
   5.1. What are Licensing Authorities? 41
   5.2. The Jurisdiction of Licensing Authorities 42
   5.3. How Licensing Authorities Work 42

5.4. The Relationship Between Licensing Authorities and the Four Licensing Objectives 42

5.5. The Four Licensing Objectives: 42

5.6. How Must Licensing Authorities Promote the Licensing Objectives? 43

5.7. The Licensing Policy Statement 44

5.8. Guidance Issued by the Secretary of State 45

5.9. Duties of the Licensing Authority 45

5.10. Licensing Authorities Review Questions 49

6. The Personal Licence 51

6.1. What is a Personal Licence? 51

6.2. How Long is a Personal Licence Valid? 52

6.3. Who is a Personal Licence Granted by? 52

6.4. How to apply for a Personal Licence 52

6.5. The Personal Licence Application Criteria - Eligibility 55

6.6. Police Objection to the Personal Licence Application - the 14 Day Rule 57

6.7. Determination of Application 58

6.8. Consequences of Conviction for a Relevant Offence After Grant of Licence - Forfeiture or Suspension 58

6.9. Personal Licence Review Questions 59

7. The Five Duties of the Personal Licence Holder 61

7.1. Duty One: To Provide Changes in Name and Address 61

7.2. Duty Two: To Produce a Licence Upon Request 61

7.3. Duty Three: To Disclose Criminal Convictions Whilst the Application Process is Ongoing 62

7.4. Duty Four: To Disclose an Offence After Grant of a Personal Licence 62

7.5. Duty Five: to Inform a Magistrates Court of a Personal Licence When Charged with a Relevant Offence 63

7.6. Reporting a Lost or Stolen Personal Licence 63

7.7. The 5 Duties of the Personal Licence Holder - Review Questions .. 64

8. The Premises Licence 65

    8.1. What is a Premises Licence? 65

    8.2. What are Licensable Activities? 65

    8.3. Mandatory Conditions on a Premises Licence 66

    8.4. The Designated Premises Supervisor (DPS) 68

    8.5. The Responsibilities of the Designated Premises Supervisor (DPS) 68

    8.6. What is an Operating Schedule? 69

    8.7. The Premises Licence Application Procedure 71

    8.8. Obtaining Advance Consent for a Premises Licence Where the Premises are Under Construction/Alteration - the Provisional Statement 73

    8.9. What Happens When a Premises Licence Holder Dies, Becomes Insolvent or Incapacitated? - the Interim Authority Notice 74

    8.10. Premises Licence Reviews 74

    8.11. Premises Licence Review Questions 76

9. The Club Premises Certificate 79

    9.1. Qualifying Club Criteria 79

    9.2. Qualifying Club Activities - What Are They? 80

    9.3. What Are The Benefits of Holding a Club Premises Certificate? 80

    9.4. Applying for a Club Premises Certificate 81

    9.5. Clubs and Right of Entry 82

    9.6. The Club Certificate Review Questions 83

10. The Temporary Events Notice ('TEN') 85

    10.1. In What Circumstances Would a 'TEN' be Required? 86

    10.2. How is a Temporary Activity Defined 87

    10.3. Temporary Events Notice (TEN) Applications 88

    10.4. The Community and Ancillary Sellers Notice (CAN) 90

10.5. TEN Review Questions 91

11. Suspension and Closure - Police Powers 93

    11.1. Police Power to Close all Premises in an Area Experiencing Disorder 93

    11.2. Police Closure Order for Specified Premises 94

    11.3. Conduct of the Premises Licence Holder 95

    11.4. Extension and Cancellation of Closure Orders 95

    11.5. Application to the Magistrates' Court by Police 95

    11.6. Consideration of Closure Orders by the Magistrates' Court 96

    11.7. Appeals Against the Decision of the Magistrates' Court 96

    11.8. Review of a Premises Licence Following a Closure Order 96

    11.9. Extended Closure Powers: Anti-Social Behaviour Act 2003 97

    11.10. Extended Closure Powers: Violent Crime Reduction Act 2006 ... 97

    11.11. Suspension and Closure - Police Powers Review Questions 98

12. Closure Powers - The Local Authority 101

    12.1. Closure by the Local Authority 101

    12.2. Delegation of Closure Powers to Environmental Health Officers (EHO) 102

    12.3. Closure Powers - The Local Authority Review Questions 103

13. Right of Entry to Licensed Premises 105

    13.1. Who has the Right of Entry to Licensed Premises and When? 105

    13.2. Rights of Entry to Licensed Premises Review Questions 107

14. Illegal Drugs, Smoking and Disorderly Conduct 109

    14.1. Illegal Drug Use 109

    14.2. Smoking on Licensed Premises 112

    14.3. Disorderly Conduct on Licensed Premises 113

    14.4. Illegal Drugs, Smoking and Disorderly Conduct Review Questions 115

15. The First Licensing Objective: Prevention of Crime and Disorder 117

- 15.1. Community Safety Partnerships 118
- 15.2. Principles of Preventing Crime and Disorder 118
- 15.3. Voluntary Partnership Schemes 121
- 15.4. Responsible Drinks Promotions and the Consequences of Irresponsible Promotions 122
- 15.5. Irresponsible Drinks Promotions 125
- 15.6. Penalties Relating to Disorderly Conduct on Licensed Premises . 126
- 15.7. The First Licensing Objective: Prevention of Crime and Disorder Review Questions 127

16. The Second Licensing Objective: Public Safety 129
- 16.1. The Regulatory Reform (Fire Safety) Order 2005 - Fire Risk Assessment 129
- 16.2. Control of Noise at Work Regulations 2005 - Noise Risk Assessments 130
- 16.3. Other Public Safety Measures 131
- 16.4. The New 'Health-Related' Objective 132
- 16.5. The Second Licensing Objective: Public Safety Review Questions 134

17. The Third Licensing Objective - Prevention of Public Nuisance 135
- 17.1. How is Public Nuisance defined? 135
- 17.2. Penalties for Breach of Public Nuisance 136
- 17.3. The Third Licensing Objective: Prevention of Public Nuisance Review Questions 137

18. The Fourth Licensing Objective: Protection of Children 139
- 18.1. Sale of Alcohol to Young Persons 139
- 18.2. Sale of Liqueur Confectionery to Children 140
- 18.3. Defences to the Above Offences – The Age Verification Policy . 140
- 18.4. The Proof of Age Standards Scheme 141
- 18.5. Prohibition of Unsupervised Sales by Children 142

18.6. Purchase of Alcohol by Young Persons 142

18.7. Test Purchasing 143

18.8. Consumption of Alcohol by Young Persons 143

18.9. Delivering Alcohol to Children 143

18.10. Sending a Child to Obtain Alcohol 144

18.11. Allowing Children on to Licensed Premises 144

18.12. Penalties for Breach 145

18.13. The Fourth Licensing Objective: Protection of Children Review Questions 146

19. Hearings and Appeals 149

19.1. Licensing Committees 149

19.2. The Purpose and Procedures of Licensing Hearings 149

19.3. Delegation of Functions 150

19.4. Licensing Hearings 150

19.5. The Licensing Appeal Procedure 152

19.6. Hearings and Appeals Review Questions 153

20. Quiz Answers 155

1. OVERVIEW OF THE LEVEL 2 APLH LICENSING MANUAL

This Licensing Manual is designed to give you a thorough understanding of alcohol licensing as prescribed by the Licensing Act 2003 and subsequent legislation up to and including the Police Reform and Social Responsibility Act 2011.

This manual is intended to be fully comprehensive and as such, to act as a reference guide throughout your career as a personal licence holder. However, some pieces of information in the manual are more critical for the personal licence examination than others. These are highlighted in *italics.*

Pro-Leagle and Pro-Leagle Wired also provide a variety of licensing services. Learn more at: *http://www.proleagle.com.* Alternatively, email Pro-Leagle at: *info@proleagle.com.*

An executive summary of the manual's contents is as follows:

2. Introduction

The old licensing regime is briefly discussed before introduction of the new unified system under the Licensing Act 2003.

3. Licensable Activities

This section discusses in detail the scope of licensable activities under the Licensing Act 2003, explains what is meant by 'sale by retail of alcohol' and takes a closer look at the defence of 'due diligence' for unauthorised licensable activities.

4. Alcohol in a Nutshell

The legal categorisation of alcoholic drinks is clearly defined prior to a discussion of the physiological effects of alcohol and how it is absorbed and excreted.

5. Licensing Authorities

Licensing Authorities, how they operate and the extent of their jurisdiction in England and Wales are discussed. An overview of the four Licensing Objectives is also provided and the relationship between the Licensing Authorities and these Objectives delineated.

6. The Personal Licence

This section sets out the nature of a personal licence, the application process for obtaining one and any objections which may be raised, particularly by the police. It also discusses forfeiture and recent changes to renewal of a personal licence.

7. The Five Duties of the Personal Licence Holder

The Five statutory duties of the personal licence holder are clarified and the penalties for failing to comply with these duties are outlined.

8. Premises Licence

This section sets out what a premises licence is, the process of obtaining one and the objections which may be raised. It also outlines the responsibilities of a Designated Premises Supervisor (DPS) and the significance of a Provisional Statement and an Interim Authority Notice.

9. Club Premises Certificates

The three qualifying Club Activities are illustrated and a brief outline of how a Club Premises Certificate can be obtained and operated under is provided.

10. The Temporary Events Notice ('TEN')

This section highlights activities within the remit of a TEN for those who hold a personal licence and those who do not. It also discusses police objections and any modifications that may be required before the TEN is granted.

11. Suspension And Closure - Police Powers

The powers the police have to suspend a personal licence and close licensed premises, are discussed in conjunction with the repercussions should this occur.

12. Closure Powers - The Local Authority

The powers the local authority has to close licensed premises are detailed.

13. Right of Entry to Licensed Premises

This section sets out who is entitled to enter licensed premises at 'all reasonable times' - both during the premises licence application process and once it has been granted.

14. Illegal Drugs, Smoking and Disorderly Conduct

The most common illegal drugs likely to be found on licensed premises are discussed alongside measures to discourage and detect illegal drug use. This section also outlines what conduct can be regarded as 'disorderly', who can be charged with the offence of disorderly conduct and the offences of disorderly conduct that can be committed.

15. The First Licensing Objective - Prevention of Crime and Disorder

The importance of local partnership initiatives, such as Community Safety Partnerships, is discussed as well as the importance of taking a proactive yet sensitive approach to operating safe and well managed licensed premises.

16. The Second Licensing Objective - Public Safety

This section outlines what is meant by Public Safety and its significance to licensed premises.

17. The Third Licensing Objective - Prevention of Public Nuisance

This section demystifies the broad meaning of public nuisance, despite its lack of clear definition in the Licensing Act 2003, and highlights the importance of monitoring noise levels and odours on a continual basis.

18. The Fourth Licensing Objective - Protection of Children

The legal definition of 'children' is given and the necessity for identity checks to ascertain age discussed. Also covered is the use of Test Purchasing by local authorities to monitor licensed premises for underage sales of alcohol. In addition, the two defences to criminal charges involving alcohol and children are outlined.

19. Hearings and Appeals

This section deals with the determination of applications for personal licences, premises licences, club certificates and Temporary Event Notices by the local Licensing Authority. Appeals against decisions of the Licensing Authority are also covered.

2. INTRODUCTION

2.1. The Licensing Act - the New Regime

When the Licensing Act 2003 received royal assent on 10 July 2003 it was considered the most far-reaching reform of licensing in over 100 years. Gone were the Licensing Justices, grandfather rights and a mishmash of old-fashioned legislation containing antiquated controls.

The new law heralded a completely new system of licensing that integrated the sale and supply of alcohol, public entertainment, and the provision of late-night refreshment under a single licensing regime.

Pubs, clubs, bars, restaurants, off-licences, stores and superstores, cinemas, theatres, village and community halls and premises (including vehicles) selling hot food and hot drinks between 11:00pm and 5:00am now fall within the new licensing system.

Responsibility for this new system of licensing was transferred from the Licensing Justices and the Court system to local authorities under the guidance of the Secretary of State in central government.

2. Introduction

In a nutshell, the Licensing Act 2003 attempts to balance new rights and freedoms for licence holders (such as the extension of opening hours) with new powers for the local police and Licensing Authorities. The principle aims of the Act are to control alcohol abuse and to seek to reduce alcohol-fuelled crime.

The introduction of the Licensing Act 2003 and supporting regulations has resulted in a consolidation of licensing law. These changes are included in the following statutes, regulations and guidances:

- The Licensing Act 2003
- The Licensing Act 2003 (Premises Licences and Club Premises Certificates) Regulations 2005
- The Licensing Act 2003 (Permitted Temporary Activity (Notices) Regulations 2005
- Temporary Event Notice Regulatory Impact Assessment
- The Licensing Act 2003 (Personal Licences) Regulations 2005
- The Licensing Act 2003 (Transitional Provisions) Order 2005
- The Licensing Act 2003 (Personal Licences: Relevant Offences (Amendment)) Order 2005
- The Licensing Act 2003 (Hearings) Regulations 2005
- The Licensing Act 2003 Licensing Authority's Register (other information) Regulations 2005
- Regulatory Impact Assessment
- The Licensing Act 2003 (Fees) Regulations 2005

Licensing legislation is in a process of continuous evolution. New or modified measures have been introduced by a variety of Acts and Orders post the 2003 Act. These include, but are not limited to, the:

- Anti-Social Behaviour Act 2003
- Clean Neighbourhoods and Environment Act 2005
- Health Act 2006
- Police and Justice Act 2006
- Violent Crime Reduction Act 2006
- Police and Crime Act 2009
- Police Reform and Social Responsibility Act 2011

- Live Music Act 2012
- Legal Aid, Sentencing and Punishment of Offenders Act 2012
- Licensing Act 2003 (Descriptions of Entertainment) (Amendment) Order 2013
- The Legislative Reform (Entertainment Licensing) Order 2014
- The Deregulation Act 2015
- The Immigration Act 2016
- The Policing & Crime Act 2017
- Licensing Act 2003 (Miscellaneous Amendments) Regulations 2017

3. Licensable Activities

There are two types of licences under the Licensing Act 2003.

1. A *personal licence* is held by an individual and enables them to sell alcohol in licensed premises.

2. A *premises licence* authorises a premises to be used for one or more licensable activities.

Both licences must be in place for the sale of alcohol to be legal.

The only current exception is where the licensing activity is intended to be temporary. In this case it is possible to apply for a Temporary Event Notice (otherwise known as 'TEN'). Community and Ancillary Sellers Notices (CANs) may, or may not, also be a future option (see Section 10).

The Licensing Act 2003 states four key licensable activities that are regulated by local authorities. These are set out below.

The four Licensable activities are -

1. ***The sale by retail of alcohol***
2. ***The supply of alcohol on behalf of a club to a club member***
3. ***The provision of regulated entertainment and***
4. ***The provision of late-night refreshment***

3.1. The Sale By Retail of Alcohol

Under the Licensing Act 2003, 'sale by retail' means all sale of alcohol to the public, irrespective of quantity. The only exceptions are sale of alcohol for trade purposes (to another personal licence holder for their business) or supply of alcohol in a members club.

Charity events, where alcohol is either included in the ticket price or is supplied in return for unspecified donations, also fall within the definition of 'sale by retail' of alcohol.

In order for alcohol to be sold to the public the premises must be covered by a premises licence, there must be a Designated Premises Supervisor (DPS) and at least one personal licence holder. The premises licence holder may be the DPS. The personal licence holder who actually authorises sale of alcohol can also be the DPS, but does not have to be.

3.1.1. Internet and mail order sales

A call centre receiving alcohol orders by internet, phone or mail order does not require a premises licence or a personal licence holder to authorise sales. This is because the call centre is not considered to be the point of sale. Under the regulations, **the point of sale is the warehouse from which the order is dispatched**. Both a premises licence and a Designated Premises Supervisor will be required for the warehouse to legally sell alcohol.

3.1.2. Moving vehicles, garages and motorway service stations

It is against the law to sell alcohol from a moving vehicle such as a van. The vehicle must be parked. This offence could result in a penalty of **3 months in prison and/or an unlimited fine**. Alcohol cannot be sold at garages that only sell fuel. If a garage sells other goods such as groceries it may be considered for a premises licence. Alcohol can also not *normally* be sold at motorway service areas. However, the fine print of Section 176 of the Licensing Act 2003 limits this restriction to Government-owned service stations. Theoretically, privately-owned service areas can sell alcohol provided that a premises licence can be obtained from the local council. As of January 2014, several such service areas have done just that - the most extreme example being the opening of a JD Wetherspoon public house, The Hope & Champion, at the Extra Motorway Service Area at junction 2 of the M40 in Beaconsfield, Buckinghamshire.

Following the 2012-2013 Alcohol Strategy Consultation it was recognised that this regulatory approach was inconsistent and that there was a need to clarify the law. It is possible therefore that wider sale of alcohol at motorway service areas may be approved in the future.

3.2. When Will You be Exempt from Requiring a Licence to Sell Alcohol? - The Seven Exemptions

Exemption 1: Where the sale of alcohol is purely *business to business*

Supply of any amount of alcohol for trade purposes to a licensed premises or to a premises user with a Temporary Event Notice (TEN), is now considered to be a business to business transaction and is exempt from licensing. Trade sales were previously defined as large volume, or wholesale, transactions. The Licensing Act 2003 does not provide a definition of wholesale quantity. This is because such a definition is now obsolete.

Conversely all sales of alcohol to a member of their public for their own consumption, whatever the quantity, now require a licence.

Exemption 2: Prizes of alcohol in *raffles and tombolas*

The issue of prizes of alcohol in small raffles or tombolas was a cause for concern under the Licensing Act 1964. At that time, a licence was needed whenever a ticket conveying a chance to win alcohol was sold. This was because it could be argued that sale or supply of alcohol had taken place. This placed an unfair burden on small organisations and charities who were sometimes accused of breaking licensing law.

You are now permitted to sell alcohol without a licence in a raffle or tombola as long as you adhere to the following conditions:

- The financial proceeds of the entertainment and raffle (after deduction of expenses) are not to be used for private gain
- The alcohol must be supplied in sealed containers.
- There must be no monetary prizes.

- Tickets are to be sold on the premises, during the entertainment, and the raffle must be drawn during the event
- The lottery must be promoted as an incident of exempt entertainment.
- Participating in the lottery, or in gaming, must not be the main inducement to attend the entertainment.

Exemption 3: Alcohol sold on *certain waterways*

You are permitted to sell alcohol without a licence aboard:

- A hovercraft.
- A vessel engaged on an international journey.
- At an approved wharf at a designated port or hover port.

Exemption 4: Alcohol sold at a *royal palace*

Exemption 5: Alcohol sold at a *designated airport* - beyond the check-in within a duty free area or on an *aeroplane on a journey*

Exemption 6: Alcohol sold at *premises occupied by the armed forces* or exempt on the grounds of national security

Exemption 7: Exemptions for *performers* in the provision of regulated entertainment

The Licensing Act 2003 protects performers of regulated entertainment from prosecution if they participate in any unauthorised, licensable activity. A person does not commit an offence if they:

- Perform a play
- Participate as a sportsman in an indoor sporting event
- Box or wrestle in a regulated boxing or wrestling event
- Perform live music
- Play recorded music
- Perform dance
- Perform something similar to music, dance etc.

The Act seeks to penalise those who *organise or carry out such activities rather than the performers themselves*.

3.3. The Supply of Alcohol on Behalf of a Club to a Club Member

A 'club' means premises such as a Conservative Club or a social club where the alcohol is owned by the members. As the members already own the alcohol it is not sold, but is considered to be supplied to the members.

A club premises certificate is required for supply of alcohol in a club, but neither a personal nor premises licence is required.

3.4. Provision of Late Night Refreshment

A premises licence is required for supply of hot food or drink to the public between **11pm and 5am**. A personal licence is only required if alcohol is sold. These restrictions apply to supply of food for consumption both on and of the premises. They affect, for example, local takeaways open late at night. Automatic drinks dispensers providing hot drinks are not included. Vending machines providing hot food are included, even if no staff intervention is required.

Following the 2012-2013 Alcohol Strategy Consultation the Government expressed a desire to free up businesses that provide late night refreshment by removing the requirement to have a licence where there is no need for one. Section 71 of the Deregulation Act 2015 plans to enable Local Authorities to make **specific exemptions from late night refreshment licensing** based on local knowledge. Such exemptions will apply to particular locations, types of premises, or specific periods of time (beginning no earlier than 11pm and ending no later than 5am). The commencement of section 71 will require secondary legislation.

3.5. The Provision of Regulated Entertainment

The provision of regulated entertainment covers the provision of entertainment such as film, music, theatre, dance or sport. The original definitions of regulated entertainment in the Licensing Act 2003 have been modified by the Live Music Act 2012, Licensing Act 2003 (Descriptions of Entertainment) (Amendment) Order 2013, The Legislative Reform (Entertainment Licensing) Order 2014 and the Deregulation Act 2015.

It is important that the correct licensing of regulated entertainment is not overlooked. As discussed later, noise generated by regulated entertainment can generate complaints from local residents which in turn can endanger the successful operation of the business.

To be licensable, an activity needs to be, at least partly, provided for the purpose of entertaining an audience. It has to be held on premises made available for the purpose of enabling that activity; and must take place in the presence of a public audience, or if the activity takes place in private, be the subject of a charge made with a view to profit.

A licence for regulated entertainment is always required for **entertainment activities that take place before 8am or after 11pm**, unless exempted under any other provision of the Licensing Act 2003 as amended. Regulated entertainment is classified as follows:

- **The performance of a play or a performance of dance**
  - *No licence is required for performances of theatre or dance between **8am and 11pm** on any day, provided that the audience does not exceed **500**.*

- **An exhibition of a film**
  - *No licence is required for '**not-for-profit**' film exhibitions held in community premises (such as church or village halls) between **8am and 11pm** on any day, provided that the audience does not exceed **500**, age classification ratings are complied with and that consent is obtained from the person/body responsible for the premises.*

- **An indoor sporting event**
  - *No licence is required for performances of theatre or dance between **8am and 11pm** on any day, provided that those present do not exceed **1000**.*

- **Boxing or wrestling entertainment**
  - *No licence is required for Greco-Roman or freestyle wrestling between two participants (regardless of gender). To be exempt, the entertainment must take place wholly inside a building in front of no more than **1000** spectators. The entertainment must take place between **8am and 11pm on the same day**.*

- **Any playing of recorded music or the performance of live music**

  The following is exempt **between 8am and 11pm** *on any day:*

  - *A performance of* **unamplified live music** *on any premises.*

  The following is exempt **between 8am and 11pm** *with the additional condition of an* **audience limit of 500**:

  - *A performance of* **amplified live music in a workplace** *that is not licensed to sell alcohol on those premises.*
  - *A performance of* **amplified live music or recorded music on premises authorised to sell alcohol** *for consumption on those premises.*
  - *A performance of* **amplified live music or recorded music in a community premises** *not licensed to sell alcohol (such as a church or village hall) or at the non-residential premises of a* **local authority**, **school**, *or* **hospital** *provided that the organiser gets consent for the performance from the person/body who is responsible for the premises.*

- **Entertainment of a similar description to live/recorded music or dance**

3.5.1. Specific Regulated Entertainment Exemptions

There are several exemptions from the requirement of a premises licence when providing regulated entertainment. However, if alcohol is to be supplied, or regulated late night refreshment provided, a licence will still be required for those activities. The main exemptions are as follows:

- **Activities in places of public religious worship** or which involve an act of worship in a religious context;
- **Teaching students to perform music or to dance**;
- **The demonstration of a product** – for example, a guitar – in a music shop;
- **The rehearsal of a play or performance of music for a private audience** where no charge is made with a view to making a profit;
- **Morris dancing** (or similar)

- ***Incidental music or film*** – the performance of live music, the playing of recorded music or an exhibition of moving pictures if it is incidental to some other activity;
- ***A spontaneous performance*** of music, singing or dancing;
- ***Garden fetes*** – or similar if not being promoted or held for purposes of private gain;
- ***Films for advertisement, information, education*** or in museums or art galleries;
- ***Television or radio broadcasts*** – as long as the programme is live and simultaneous;
- ***Vehicles in motion*** – at a time when the vehicle is not permanently or temporarily parked;
- ***Games played in pubs, youth clubs etc.*** (e.g. pool, darts and table tennis);
- ***Stand-up comedy***; and
- ***Provision of entertainment facilities*** (e.g. dance floors).

3.5.2. 'Cross-Activity' Regulated Entertainment Exemptions

The following Cross-Activity exemptions (exempting more than one form of regulated activity from licensing) have been introduced by legislative reform with **no limit on audience size**.

- *Entertainment **provided by, or on behalf of,** health care providers, local authorities and school proprietors* is no longer regarded as regulated so long as it takes place at their own defined (non-domestic) premises **between 8am and 11pm**.

- *Entertainment provided by travelling circuses* - taking place wholly within a moveable structure which cannot remain on the same site for more than **28 days**. The entertainment must not comprise regulated exhibition of film or regulated boxing/wrestling

3.6. Unauthorised Licensable Activities

Section 136 of the Licensing Act 2003 makes it an offence to carry on or to attempt to carry on a licensable activity without the authorisation of:

1. A premises licence,
2. A club premises certificate
3. A Temporary Event Notice

3.6.1. Penalties for selling alcohol without a personal licence

A person commits an offence if they sell alcohol without either a personal licence or the authorisation of a person holding such a licence.

A person guilty of this offence is liable on summary conviction to imprisonment for a term not exceeding **six months** or to **an unlimited fine**, or to both.

A court that convicts a person of selling alcohol without the authority of a personal licence holder may order the alcohol in question to be forfeited. The alcohol will either be destroyed or dealt with in such manner as the court may decide.

3.6.2. Offence of keeping alcohol on the premises with an intention of sale by retail without a licence.

Section 138 of the Licensing Act 2003 makes it an offence to keep alcohol on the premises if the intention is to sell it to the general public and an appropriate licence is not in place.

3.6.3. Offence of keeping smuggled alcohol on licensed premises

It is also an offence to keep smuggled alcohol on licensed premises. On conviction, such goods may be confiscated. Persons liable for such offences include anyone working on the premises, paid or unpaid, who is in a position to prevent the offence from taking place.

3.6.4. The defence of 'due diligence'

A defence of 'due diligence' is available to someone charged with the above offences if both of the following are true:

1. Their act was due to a mistake. This mistake may involve reliance on inaccurate information given by another person or to an act or omission by another person. Alternatively it may relate to some other cause beyond their control.

2. They took all reasonable precautions and exercised all due diligence to avoid committing the offence.

3.7. Licensable Activities Review Questions

See section 20 for answers

1. What does 'Sale by Retail' mean?

(A) The sale of alcohol to a trader for the purposes of their trade

(B) Any sale of alcohol to any person for their own consumption

(C) The sale of spirits in imperial measures

(D) Giving an alcoholic drink away for no charge

2. Which of the following is NOT classed as Regulated Entertainment?

(A) A dance marathon for charity

(B) Traditional folk dancing

(C) A talent competition

(D) A karaoke evening

3. Which of these is NOT considered to be regulated entertainment?

(A) A choir singing at a place of worship

(B) A theatre production

(C) A four piece band in a public house

(D) A film showing at a cinema

4. Which of these locations is exempt from the licensing provisions of the Licensing Act 2003?

(A) Aboard a ship on an international journey

(B) A canal boat

(C) A converted barn

(D) A grade 'A' listed castle

5. **What may be the sentence for carrying out unauthorised licensable activities?**

(A) Imprisonment for a term not exceeding six months

(B) A fine not exceeding £20,000

(C) A lifetime ban on supplying licensable activities to the public

(D) Imprisonment for a term not exceeding six months and/or an unlimited fine

4. Alcohol in a Nutshell

Alcohol is defined under Section 191 of the Licensing Act 2003 as spirits, wine, beer, cider or any other fermented, distilled or spirit liqueur except:

- ***Alcohol with strength below 0.5%***
- Perfume
- Flavouring essences and Angostura bitters
- Denatured alcohol (methylated spirits) or methyl alcohol
- Naphtha

Section 135 of the Policing and Crime Act 2017 amended the definition of "alcohol" provided in the Licensing Act 2003 to include alcohol "in any state." This will mean powdered and vapourised alcohol is also now regulated under the Licensing Act 2003.

4. Alcohol in a Nutshell

4.1. Alcoholic Strength and 'ABV'

The greater the amount of alcohol as a percentage of the total volume of a drink, the stronger and more intoxicating the drink. This measurement of alcoholic strength is called 'alcohol by volume' or 'ABV'.

Some examples:

Beers: if beer is labelled as 3.5% ABV, then this means that 3.5% of the beer is pure alcohol. There are over 1,000 beers and ciders on sale in the UK and most have an ABV of between 3% and 5%. Notable exceptions of beers with an extremely high alcohol content include Gold Label (Interbrew) 9.5% ABV, Christmas Noggin (Hoskins & Oldfield) 10% ABV, Harvest Ale (JW Lees) 11.5% ABV and Ramsey Ruin (Payn Brewery) 13% ABV.

Vodka: if vodka is labelled as 37.5% ABV then this means that 37.5% of the vodka is pure alcohol. Most spirits have an ABV of 35-40%.

Wines: if wine is labelled as 12% ABV, this means that 12% of a glass, bottle or carafe of wine is pure alcohol. Wines range from 9%-16% ABV.

4.2. How do you Calculate Units of Alcohol?

To assist customers in monitoring their alcoholic intake you need to be able to calculate the amount of alcohol contained in different drinks.

This is achieved by counting the number of 'units of alcohol' in a particular drink. *A 'unit' is 8 grams (g) or 10 millilitres (ml) of alcohol.* To calculate the number of units of alcohol in a given quantity of any drink you apply the following formula:

Quantity of liquid (ml) x %ABV x 0.001

OR *(Volume (ml) x %ABV) divided by 1000*

Examples:

One pint of beer (568 ml) at 5%ABV = 2.84 units
(568 x 5 x 0.001 = 2.84 units)
125 ml of wine at 16% ABV = 2 units
(125 x 16 x 0.001 = 2 units)
25 ml of whisky at 37.5%ABV = 0.9 units
(25 x 37.5 x 0.001 = 0.9 units)

4.3. Labelling Laws for Alcoholic Drinks - Clear Labelling of Strength (ABV) Required

Packaged drinks with an ABV of *more than 1.2%* must be labelled with their alcoholic content by volume. Draught products usually have the ABV stated on the invoice or on the brewery product or stock list. They may also be shown on the front label. The ABV must be shown on the price list. Cocktails and other mixed drinks are excluded from this requirement.

Specified descriptions can be used to describe drinks of not more than 1.2% ABV. These descriptions include:

- *'low alcohol'* - drinks with alcoholic strength by volume of *not more than 1.2%*

- *'de-alcoholised'* - drinks from which the alcohol has been extracted and which have an alcoholic strength by volume of *not more than 0.5%*, and

- *'alcohol-free'* - a drink from which the alcohol has been extracted and which has an alcoholic strength by volume of *not more than 0.05%*.

Customers may be confused about the difference between 'no-alcohol' and 'low-alcohol' beers. The premises supervisor and staff however must understand the difference.

4.4. Physiological Effects of Alcohol

4.4.1. The physical effects of alcohol

Alcohol is a depressant that slows down brain activity. Whilst one or two drinks makes most people feel relaxed, more alcohol may cause feelings of anxiety, depression, and often aggression. Physical skills such as those required for driving, the ability to reason and emotional inhibitions, are all reduced by the consumption of alcohol.

4.4.2. The Correlation Between Units of Alcohol and Behaviour

1-3 units

Drinkers become more active, and feel more alert and cheerful. Many people find it easier to socialise and talk to others. The pulse rate and breathing quicken, and the veins widen.

4-7 units

The alert and relaxed state continues, but judging situations becomes more difficult. Everyday actions seem to become easier (such as driving), but more mistakes are made as reaction times are increased and the angle of vision begins to decrease.

8-10 units

Drinkers become careless and silly. They do things they would not normally do when sober. Cheerfulness can turn to depression, and they find it more difficult to control aggression, leading to an increased tendency to get into brawls and fights.

10 units+

Motions and movements become awkward and the drinker may become increasingly violent. Seeing, walking and talking all become more difficult. Drinkers do things without conscious knowledge. Stupor, unconsciousness and even death can result from this level of intoxication. Coma stage may occur when the blood alcohol content (BAC) rises above ***350 milligrams of alcohol per 100ml of blood (0.35%)***. Excessive alcohol intake can, in extreme cases, suppress heart rate and inhibit breathing. This can result in coma and death.

4.4.3. Absorption of alcohol into the bloodstream

Alcohol is absorbed into the bloodstream through the stomach and reaches all parts of the body. The effect that alcohol has on an individual depends directly on how much alcohol is in the bloodstream at any one time, in other words the 'blood-alcohol content' (BAC).

BAC is measured in terms of milligrams (mg) of alcohol in milliliters (ml) of blood.

A BAC of ***80 mg of alcohol in 100 ml of blood*** (otherwise referred to as 0.08%) is the level above which it is an offence to drive. Measured on a breathalyser, this equates to ***35 microgrammes (µg) of alcohol in 100 ml of breath***.

The amount of alcohol in the bloodstream and the speed with which it gets there are dependent on a number of factors. Among these are:

- ***Alcohol content*** - drinking strong drinks quickly leads to a high blood alcohol level.

- ***Physical size*** - a small person has less blood than a large person. A single drink will hence result in a higher blood alcohol concentration in a small person than in a large one

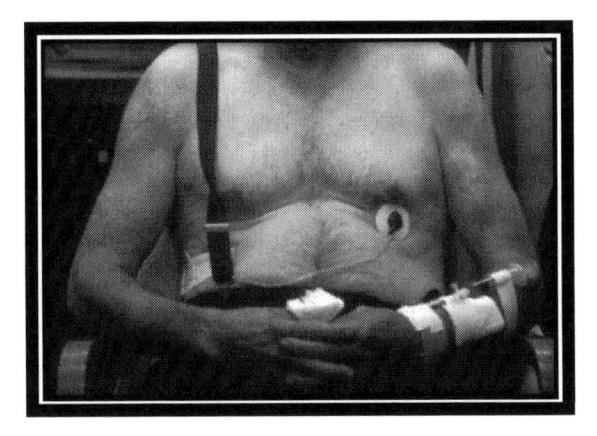

- ***Gender*** - the same drinks will produce a higher concentration of alcohol in the blood of a woman than in a man. This is because women have fewer gastric (stomach) enzymes than men to break down the alcohol before it enters the bloodstream. Women also tend to have lower body water content than men. Alcohol is hence less diluted than in men leading to a higher concentration of alcohol in the bloodstream

- ***Food consumed*** - food in the stomach slows down the rate at which alcohol enters the bloodstream. This reduces the peak alcohol levels in the blood. It does not prevent alcohol absorption however

As a licence holder you have to use your common sense, experience and observation to judge whether someone has become drunk. Behaviour may progress through being 'merry' to displaying slurred speech, loss of physical coordination, aggressiveness or a tendency to become maudlin, and finally, unconsciousness. **Remember that it is an offence to sell alcohol to someone who is drunk.**

4.4.4. Elimination of alcohol from the body

When a person stops drinking, body alcohol content (BAC) starts to fall. ***The liver removes most of the alcohol*** as the blood circulates through it. In addition ***some alcohol is lost through the lungs or in the urine***. Approximately ***one hour is needed to eliminate one unit of alcohol*** from the body, and ***there is no way this can be speeded up***. Drinking black coffee may combat the drowsiness caused by alcohol, because of the caffeine in the coffee, but it will not speed up the drinker's metabolic processes.

4.5. Sensible Drinking and Health Benefits

Moderate drinking in appropriate circumstances presents little or no harm to the drinker and can even provide health benefits. The medically recommended number of units of alcohol per week is **14 for women and 21 for men**. The following advice is based on the UK Government's sensible drinking message:

Men: Most men can drink up to three to four units of alcohol a day without significant risks to their health. Surprisingly, evidence shows that drinking up to one or two units a day for men aged 40 can reduce the risks of coronary heart disease.

Women: Who are trying to conceive or who are pregnant should avoid getting drunk and are advised to consume no more than one or two units of alcohol once or twice a week. After the menopause there is evidence that drinking one or two units a day, but no more, can protect against coronary heart disease.

4.5.1. Elimination of alcohol from the body

DO

- Abstain for 48 hours following an episode of heavy drinking to let your body recover
- Remember drinks poured at home are often bigger than pub measures. Work out how much you drink and try to stick to the guidelines which are daily benchmarks not weekly targets
- Get help from your doctor or a specialist agency if worried about your drinking
- Remember that drinking responsibly can be enjoyable and is compatible with a healthy lifestyle

DON'T

- Operate machinery, use electrical equipment or work at heights after drinking
- Drink before playing sports or swimming
- Drink while on certain medications - check labels and ask your doctor or pharmacist if unsure
- Binge drink - it can lead to health and other problems

4.6. Alcohol in a Nutshell Review Questions

See section 20 for answers

1. What is a unit of alcohol?

(A) 4g or 5ml of pure alcohol

(B) 8g or 10ml of pure alcohol

(C) 10g or 12ml of pure alcohol

(D) 12g or 15ml of pure alcohol

2. What is the formula for calculating the number of units in an alcoholic drink?

(A) Volume (ml) x ABV divided by 1000

(B) ABV x volume (ml) x 1000

(C) 50 divided by volume (ml) x age

(D) Age x height x weight

3. Alcoholic beverages over what percentage must be labelled with their alcoholic content?

(A) 12%

(B) 5%

(C) 1.2%

(D) 2%

4. How is alcohol absorbed into the body?

(A) Through the skin into the blood stream

(B) Through the heart into the blood stream

(C) Through the stomach into the blood stream

(D) Through the lungs into the blood stream

5. What is the definition of 'Alcohol Free' beverages?

(A) Drinks with less than 5% ABV alcohol

(B) Drinks with more than 5% ABV alcohol

(C) Drinks with no more than 0.05% ABV of alcohol

(D) Drinks containing less than half a shot of spirits

6. What is the definition of 'Low Alcohol' beverages?

(A) Drinks containing less than 2% alcohol

(B) Drinks containing less than half a shot of spirits

(C) Drinks with 'Alcopops' in the title

(D) Drinks containing no more than 1.2% ABV

5. LICENSING AUTHORITIES

The Government charges local 'Licensing Authorities' with the responsibility of administering the Licensing Act 2003.

Licensing authorities can issue personal licences, premises licences, club premises certificates, Temporary Event Notices and can also renew licences for their area.

5.1. What are Licensing Authorities?

The Licensing Authorities in England and Wales are:

- A district council in England (e.g. Lichfield district council)
- An English county council, where there is no district council (e.g. Isle of Wight)
- The council of a county or county borough in Wales
- The council of a London borough

- The common council of the City of London
- The council of the Isles of Scilly

5.2. The Jurisdiction of Licensing Authorities

Jurisdiction is defined geographically. For the purpose of the Licensing Act 2003, the geographical area over which a local Licensing Authority has jurisdiction is the same as that of the local council authority.

5.3. How Licensing Authorities Work

A Licensing Authority operates a system of control for all 'licensable activities' and 'qualifying club activities' within its area of jurisdiction. See section 3 for a summary of licensable activities. Each Licensing Authority must establish a licensing committee of between 10 and 15 members. The purpose of the licensing committee is to discharge the licensing functions of Licensing Authorities, including hearing applications and appeals but not including the publication of the licensing statement. Licensing officers may deal with some of the committee's task, such as premises and personal licence applications.

5.4. The Relationship Between Licensing Authorities and the Four Licensing Objectives

The Licensing Authorities regulate licensable activities in accordance with the Licensing Act 2003 - promoting certain fundamental objectives, known as 'the licensing objectives'. There are four of these, and they are all of equal importance. These Four Objectives are discussed in greater depth in Sections 15-18.

5.5. The Four Licensing Objectives:

The *four fundamental licensing objectives* are:
1. *The prevention of crime and disorder*
2. *The promotion of public safety*
3. *The prevention of public nuisance*
4. *The protection of children from harm*

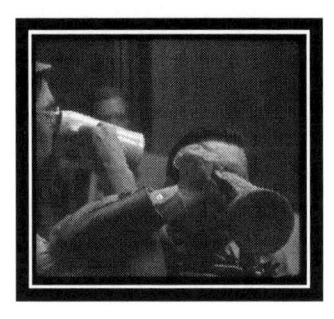

In addition, the Police Reform and Social Responsibility Act 2011 introduced a new health-related 'objective', *the prevention of harm to health*, relevant to premises licence applications falling within **Cumulative Impact areas** (those areas in which the concentration of licensed premises is considered to cause a cumulative impact on one or more of the licensing objectives).

These licensing objectives are promoted through the system of personal licences, premises licences, Temporary Event Notices, club premises certificates and licence renewals.

Conditions can be attached to premises licences in order to promote the licensing objectives. These conditions should be 'tailor-made' for each licensed premises and should not be imposed unilaterally on all premises of a given type in a given area.

5.6. How Must Licensing Authorities Promote the Licensing Objectives?

Every time a Licensing Authority considers an application for a personal licence, a premises licence, a Temporary Event Notice (TEN) or a club premises certificate, it must consider whether the application satisfies the four licensing objectives.

There are two main documents it must consult when making its decision:

1. *Its own published licensing policy statement* (Section 5 of the Licensing Act 2003).

2. *Any guidance issued by the Secretary of State* (Section 182 of the Licensing Act 2003).

Section 182 of the 2003 Act requires the Secretary of State to issue guidance to licensing authorities on the discharge of their functions under the Act. As a result of section 140 of the Policing and Crime Act 2017, the

Secretary of State will no longer have to lay this guidance before Parliament for approval before it comes into effect.

The Police Reform and Social Responsibility Act 2011 increased the remit of Licensing Authorities to reject licence applications or impose conditions on licences. Previously Licensing Authorities were only able to take a particular action if it was deemed 'necessary' for the promotion of the licensing objectives. This wording has now been amended so that **the Licensing Authority can make a decision if it is deemed 'appropriate' for the promotion of the licensing objectives.**

Determinations still have to be evidence-based and justified as being appropriate for the promotion of a licensing objective. They will also have to take into account whether any conditions being imposed can feasibly be met and the impact of the conditions on promoting other licensing objectives.

5.7. The Licensing Policy Statement

Licensing authorities are required to promote the licensing objectives. To illustrate how they promote these objectives they must publish a licensing policy. That policy runs for *five years*, although it may be reviewed or revised at any time.

Hence, in every *five year* period, each Licensing Authority must:

1. Determine its policy on how it will exercise its licensing functions, and
2. Publish a statement of that policy (a 'licensing statement') before the start of the five year period

If the Licensing Authority considers that a particular application will undermine the crime prevention objective they may refuse it. However, in relation to all the other licensing objectives the licensing policy should be non-prescriptive and should consider all applications on their individual merits. **Without a licensing policy statement an authority cannot issue any licences.**

Statements of licensing policy should not impose limits or caps on the number of licences granted in a particular area. An exception to this is where a **Cumulative Impact Policy** exists. Such policies are put in place by Licensing Authorities where the concentration of licensed premises in a specific area is considered to cause a cumulative impact on one or more of the licensing objectives. Busy city centres are prime targets for such policies - the Whiteladies Road area of Bristol for example.

Even where a Cumulative Impact Policy exists, a Licensing Authority cannot impose conditions on, or refuse to grant or vary, a premises licence or club premises certificate unless it has received a relevant representation from a responsible authority or a member of the public likely to be affected by the application.

Section 141 of the Policing and Crime Act 2017 amended the Licensing Act 2003 and put Cumulative Impact Policies on a statutory footing while introducing a requirement on licensing authorities to review the evidence on which Cumulative Impact Policies are based at least every three years.

Following the 2012-2013 Alcohol Strategy Consultation the Government introduced the concept of ***Local Alcohol Action Areas***. The Home Office and Public Health England plan to partner with local authorities in tackling alcohol-related crime and disorder in problem areas, reducing alcohol-related health harms and promoting growth by establishing vibrant night-time economies.

5.8. Guidance Issued by the Secretary of State

Government guidance to Licensing Authorities states that licensing policies must not undermine the rights of individuals to apply for, or attempt to vary the terms of, any licence allowed by the Licensing Act 2003. All applications must be considered on their merits.

It is also recognised in the government's guidance that whilst one of the main objectives of the Licensing Act 2003 is to reduce crime and disorder, there are many other instruments for doing this. Licensing policies should not attempt to control anti-social behaviour outside the control of the licensed operators of premises.

With respect to premises licence applications within Cumulative Impact Areas, applicants should be aware of the Cumulative Impact Policy, and will need to address the issues in their operating schedules in order to show that they would not add to the 'cumulative impact'.

5.9. Duties of the Licensing Authority

5.9.1. Keeping a register

Each Licensing Authority must keep a register containing:

- A record of each premises licence, club premises certificate and personal licence issued by it

- A record of each Temporary Event Notice received by it. Note that the Government originally planned to introduce a new form of licence, the Community and Ancillary Sellers Notice (CAN). These were also intended to be entered onto the Licensing Authority's register. CANs were designed to cover organisations who wished to infrequently sell small amounts of alcohol as part of a wider service in order to absolve them of the requirement to apply either for multiple TENs or a full premises licence. CANs will not, however, be introduced until such time as Section 67 of the Deregulation Act 2015 is brought into force. Currently no date is proposed for implementation..

- The matters mentioned in Schedule 3 of the Licensing Act 2003, (twenty-eight in total, pertaining mainly to applications and notices).

- Such other information as may be prescribed

Any person may inspect the Licensing Authority's register of personal licence holders **for free** so long as the inspection is **within office hours**.

5.9.2. Consultation with Government authorities - 'Responsible Authorities'

Licensing authorities must accept representations about licence applications from Responsible Authorities and deal with them appropriately. These representations may mean that a hearing is necessary to decide whether or not a licence should be granted. Examples of Responsible Authorities are as follows:

- *Police*
- *Fire Service*
- *Health and Safety Agency*
- *Local Authority Director of Public Health**
- *Environmental Health Department*
- *Planning Department*
- *Social Services department*
- *Local Trading Standards*
- *The Local Licensing Authority**

[*New in the Police Reform and Social Responsibility Act 2011]

The appointment of Licensing Authorities themselves as Responsible Authorities creates the interesting potential for a member of an authority to object to a premises licence application, or initiate a review into an existing licence, without any issues being raised by either the public or another responsible authority. The licensed trade have protested that this may lead to incidences of bias but the Government has pointed to the Gambling Act 2005 as a precedent for this type of regulation.

5.9.3. Consultation with the local community

One of the main reasons for taking licensing functions away from courts and giving them to local authorities was to ensure that licensing decisions, and those who make them, are more accountable to the general public. In particular they should be accountable to those who are most affected by licensing decisions.

Provision has therefore been made (under Section 13 of the Licensing Act 2003) for a wide range of groups and individuals to make their views known in respect of licence applications. The right to make representations was previously geographically limited to local residents and businesses '*in the vicinity*' of the relevant premises. These used to be known as '*interested parties*'.

The Police Reform and Social Responsibility Act 2011 removed this geographical restriction (and the usage of the term '*interested parties*'). Now, anyone '*likely to be affected by the application*' can make representations either for or against a licensing application. However any such objection must still relate to one or more of the licensing objectives and **must not be frivolous or vexatious**.

Note that representations from Responsible Authorities are always considered relevant and cannot be dismissed as frivolous or irrelevant.

Objections to an application may initiate a Licensing Authority Committee Hearing to decide whether the licence should be granted. It is therefore important for a licensee to establish good relations and to develop partnerships with local groups, to ensure that licensed premises are at the heart of the community and in harmony with it.

5.9.4. Input from Responsible Authorities and members of the public affected by licensing policy

Each Licensing Authority must consult with residents, businesses and Responsible Authorities within their jurisdiction when preparing its policy statement. These include the police, the local fire authority, people who represent holders of premises licences, personal licences and club premises certificates, and representatives of businesses and residents. The Licensing Authority must keep its licensing policy under review. Any revisions of that policy must be published, following consultations.

5.10. Licensing Authorities Review Questions

See section 20 for answers

1. What are Licensing Authorities?

(A) Magistrates

(B) County Court staff

(C) Bodies in England and Wales responsible for authorising Licensable Activities

(D) Other personal licence holders of 10 years or more

2. How does a Licensing Authority implement the four licensing objectives?

(A) By controlling the policing of licensed premises

(B) By enforcing the Health and Safety at Work Act 1974 on licensed premises

(C) By having responsibility for environmental health issues of all licensed premises

(D) By having a system of licensing and control of licensable activities

3. How frequently must the Licensing Authority revise is published licensing policy?

(A) Every year

(B) Every five years

(C) Every three years

(D) Every ten years

4. Who may inspect the Licensing Authority's register of personal licence holders and in what circumstances?

(A) Any person, but only by prior arrangement during office hours

(B) Any person during office hours and without payment

(C) The police and Licensing Authority personnel only

(D) Any person between 9am to 12 noon.

6. THE PERSONAL LICENCE

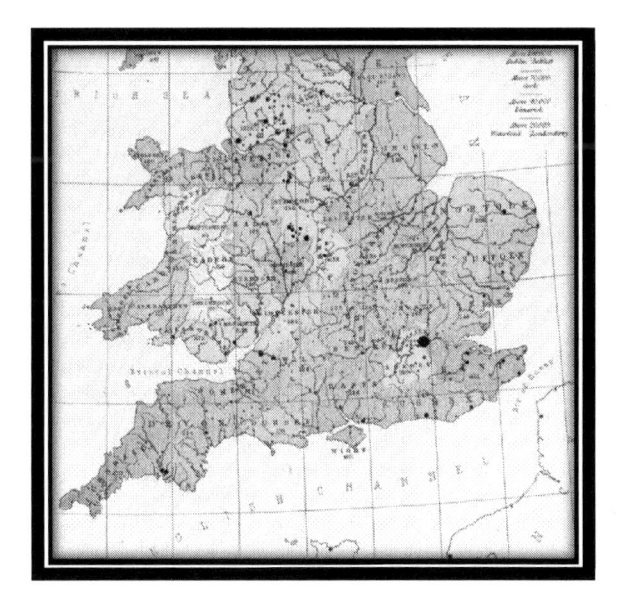

The Licensing Act 2003 separates the licensing of persons from the licensing of premises.

Most premises serving alcohol must have at least one personal licence holder (see the exceptions listed in Section 3.2 above).

A personal licence can be used throughout England and Wales. An individual can only hold one personal licence.

6.1. What is a Personal Licence?

A 'personal licence' is a licence granted to an individual that:
1. ***Enables them to sell alcohol in an off-licence of pub.*** Specifically it authorises an individual to sell alcohol by retail, or to authorise the retail sale of alcohol, in accordance with a premises licence, or

2. ***Enables them to sell alcohol in a private members club.*** Specifically, to sell alcohol by retail, supply alcohol or authorise the supply of alcohol by or on behalf of a club to, or to the order of, a member of a club

The sale or supply of alcohol in licensed premises must be made or authorised by a personal licence holder. It is therefore recommended that bar staff working on each shift are supervised by a personal licence holder.

This licence holder may or may not be the ***Designated Premises Supervisor (DPS).*** If the supervising personal licence holder is not the DPS, they should be given written authorisation by the DPS to sell or supply alcohol. Refer to Section 8.4 for further information on the DPS.

6.2. How Long is a Personal Licence Valid?

Following the 2012-2013 Alcohol Strategy Consultation the Government decided to remove the requirement to renew personal licences every 10 years. This measure was enacted 1st April 2015 via the Deregulation Act 2015. No personal licence in England and Wales expiring after 31 March 2015 needs renewal.

A personal licence cannot be used during periods of suspension which can be up to ***6 months.***

6.3. Who is a Personal Licence Granted by?

A personal licence is granted by the ***Licensing Authority in which the applicant normally resides.*** However, an application may, in any other case, be made to any other Licensing Authority.

6.4. How to apply for a Personal Licence

An individual may apply -

- For the grant of a personal licence

An application for the grant of a personal licence is normally made to the Licensing Authority for the area in which the applicant normally resides.

6.4.1. The personal licence application form

The form of application for a personal licence is prescribed by legislation and requires the applicant to provide the following information:

- His or her name (including any previous or maiden names)
- Date of birth
- Contact numbers
- Current address and, if the applicant has lived at that address for less than five years, details of previous addresses
- Previous or outstanding applications for a personal licence

6.4.2. The personal licence application form - supporting documents

The application should be accompanied by the following:

1. *Two photographs of the applicant*, one of which is endorsed as a true likeness of the applicant by a solicitor or other professional person. The photograph must be taken against a light background, be 45mm x 35mm and be full face without sunglasses, hat or other head covering (unless the applicant wears a head covering due to his or her religious beliefs). The photographs must be on photographic paper.
2. Documentary proof that the applicant has the legal right to live and work in the UK (introduced 6th April 2017 by the Immigration Act 2016).
3. A copy of the applicant's *licensing qualification*.

4. A ***criminal record check certificate*** stating that the applicant has not been convicted of a relevant or foreign offence, or where such an offence has been committed, it is disclosed on an up-to-date Criminal Record Bureau Disclosure Form.

- **Applying for a Criminal Record check with an organisation:** An applicant applying for a personal licence in response to a request from an organisation (such as a supermarket employer) can apply for a Criminal Record Check from the Criminal Records Bureau (CRB). This is done using a paper application form which is either supplied by the organisation that requested the check or provided by the CRB upon telephone confirmation by the requesting organisation. Consequently, this kind of check *cannot be obtained by an individual*.

- **Applying for a Criminal Record check as an individual:** An applicant applying as an individual in England or Wales will need to request a Basic Disclosure from Disclosure and Barring Service (DBS). The relevant body in Scotland is Disclosure Scotland, and in Northern Ireland, AccessNI.

5. The applicant is required to sign a form stating that the information contained on it is correct to the best of his or her knowledge. It is a criminal offence to make false statements on the personal licence application form.

6. The correct personal licence application fee must accompany the documents. This fee is set by Licensing Authorities and can be ascertained by individual request to a Licensing Authority.

6.5. The Personal Licence Application Criteria - Eligibility

The eligibility criteria for the grant of a personal licence are that the applicant:

- Is at least *18 years old*.
- Has the right to *live and work in the UK*.
- Possesses an *accredited qualification* or falls within an exemption as prescribed by legal statute.
- Has *not had a personal licence forfeited in the last five years*.
- Has *not been convicted of any 'relevant offences' or 'foreign offences'*

The Licensing Authority must reject the application for a personal licence if the applicant fails to meet one of the first three eligibility criteria. If the first three eligibility criteria are met but the applicant has been convicted of a 'relevant offence' or a 'foreign offence', the Licensing Authority may grant the personal licence only after consulting the police.

6.5.1. What are 'relevant offences' and 'foreign offences'?

'Relevant offences' and 'foreign offences' (as set out in Schedule 4 of the Licensing Act 2003) are offences which will prevent an individual gaining a personal licence. If such offences are committed after a licence has been granted, the licence will be revoked. With regards to drink driving, 'relevant offences' are offences under the Road Traffic Act 1988.

A 'foreign offence' means an offence under the law of any place outside England and Wales which could reasonably be considered to be equivalent to a relevant offence.

Relevant offences fall into the following categories:

- Offences under the Licensing Act 2003
- Offences under the current licensing enactments e.g. Licensing Act 1964, Late Night Refreshment Act 1969 etc.
- Offences under the Firearms Act 1968
- Offences under the Trade Descriptions Act 1968 (where goods are or include alcohol)
- Offences under the Theft act, including deception

- Offences under the Gaming Act 1968 (a child taking part in gaming on liquor-licensed premises)
- Offences under the Misuse of Drugs Act 1971
- Offences under the Theft Act 1978
- Offences under the Customs and Excise Management Act 1979
- Offences under the Tobacco Products Duty Act 1979
- Offences under the Forgery and Counterfeiting Act 1981
- Offences under the Firearms (Amendment) Act 1988
- Offences under the Copyright, Designs and Patents Act 1988
- Offences under the Road Traffic Act 1988 (drink-driving)
- Offences under the Food Safety Act
- Offences under the Trade Marks act 1994 (where goods are or include alcohol)
- Offences under the Firearms (Amendment) Act 1997
- Certain sexual offences
- Violent offences
- Offences under the Private Security Industry Act 2001
- Sexual offences listed in Schedule 3 to the Sexual Offences Act 2003
- Violent offences listed in Part 1 of Schedule 15 to the Criminal Justice Act 2003
- Offences under the Gambling Act 2005
- Offences under the Fraud Act 2006
- The manufacture, importation and sale of realistic imitation firearms contrary to section 36 of the Violent Crime Reduction Act 2006
- Using someone to mind a weapon contrary to section 28 of the Violent Crime Reduction Act 2006
- Offences under the Business Protection from Misleading Marketing Regulations 2008 (where the advertising relates to alcohol or goods that include alcohol)

- Offences under the Consumer Protection from Unfair Trading Regulations 2008 (where directly connected the promotion, sales or supply of alcohol or of a product that includes alcohol) Foreign offences are offences committed outside England and Wales that the chief officer of police in any Licensing Authority area may consider comparable to a relevant offence.
- Terrorism-related offences listed in section 41 of the Counter-terrorism Act 2008.

6.5.2. Offences which must be disregarded by the Licensing Authority

A caution is not the same as a conviction (i.e. the applicant has not been charged and convicted at Court) therefore an applicant does not need to disclose a caution as part of a personal licence application.

Convictions for relevant or foreign offences must be disregarded when the offences are 'spent offences'. Offences are 'spent' or ignored, after a 'rehabilitation period'. A rehabilitation period is a set length of time from the date of conviction. The length of the rehabilitation period depends on the original sentence given - not the offence committed.

Generally if a relevant offence does not receive a custodial sentence it **will become spent** for the purposes of the Rehabilitation of Offenders Act 1974 (c.53) **after 5 years. Spent offences do not need to be included on the application form**.

6.6. Police Objection to the Personal Licence Application - the 14 Day Rule

If a relevant or 'foreign offence' has been committed a personal licence application must be referred to the *Chief Officer of Police*. If they believe that granting a licence would undermine the prevention of crime and disorder, they **must give the Licensing Authority a Notice of Objection within 14 days** of having been notified of the licence application. In the absence of an objection, the Licensing Authority must grant the application.

When an objection is lodged by the police the Licensing Authority must hold a hearing to decide whether to reject or grant the licence. The Licensing Authority must give reasons for its decision. The need for such a hearing may be dispensed with by agreement of the authority, the applicant and the police.

6.7. Determination of Application

Provided that all the eligibility criteria listed above have been met, then an application for a personal licence will be determined in one of two ways:
1. The licence will be granted by an officer of the Licensing Authority or, if no objection to the application is received,
2. The application will be determined by the licensing committee, or a sub-committee, following a hearing at which the applicant and objectors can appear. A hearing may occur if a valid objection is made by an authority such as the police or an interested party such as local residents.

6.8. Consequences of Conviction for a Relevant Offence After Grant of Licence - Forfeiture or Suspension

When a personal licence holder is convicted of a relevant offence, the court may forfeit the personal licence, or suspend it *for up to six months*. If a licence is forfeited or suspended, the holder loses the right to authorise the retail sale or supply of alcohol.

An order to forfeit or suspend a licence may itself be suspended by the convicting court. This allows the licence to continue pending an appeal by the licence holder. This enables the licence holder to continue trading pending the outcome of an appeal.

Section 138 of the Policing and Crime Act 2017 allows licensing authorities to suspend or revoke a licence. Courts retain their existing powers. Where a licensing authority decides to suspend or revoke a licence, the licence holder will have the opportunity to make representations to the licensing committee, and will have a right to appeal to a magistrates' court.

6.9. Personal Licence Review Questions

See section 20 for answers

1. Which of the following must a personal licence application include?

(A) The correct forms, information and fee

(B) Details of any conviction pending, but only since the application

(C) Proof that a genuine offer of employment has been made to the applicant

(D) Proof that the applicant has been resident in the area for more than 6 months

2. Application for renewal of a personal licence must be made to:

(A) The authority that issued the original licence

(B) No renewal is required

(C) The authority where the applicant lives

(D) Any authority in England and Wales

3. The police must give the Licensing Authority a Notice of Objection to the grant of a personal licence within:

(A) 28 days

(B) 3 months

(C) 6 months

(D) 14 days

4. How long does a personal licence last?

(A) 10 years

(B) Indefinitely

(C) 5 years

(D) 2 years

5. How long does a personal licence last on renewal?

(A) A further 10 years

(B) No renewal is required

(C) A further 1 year

(D) It does not have to be renewed

7. THE FIVE DUTIES OF THE PERSONAL LICENCE HOLDER

7.1. Duty One: To Provide Changes in Name and Address

Section 127 of the Licensing Act 2003 requires a personal licence holder to notify the Licensing Authority as soon as possible about any change to their name or address as stated in their personal licence. This notification of name or address change must be accompanied by the personal licence or, if that is not practicable, by a statement of the reasons for the failure to provide the licence. A person commits an offence if he fails, without reasonable excuse, to comply with this requirement.

7.2. Duty Two: To Produce a Licence Upon Request

Section 135 of the Licensing Act 2003 requires a personal licence holder to produce his licence, when requested, to a police constable or to an officer of the Licensing Authority. This applies when the licence holder is on the given premises to sell, or authorise the sale of, alcohol under a premises licence or Temporary Event Notice. Failure to produce a personal licence when requested is an offence.

7.3. Duty Three: To Disclose Criminal Convictions Whilst the Application Process is Ongoing

During the licence application period an applicant must notify the Licensing Authority as soon as possible if convicted of a relevant or foreign offence. The application period begins when the application for licence grant or renewal is made and ends when the licence is either granted or withdrawn.

A person commits an offence if they fail, without reasonable excuse, to comply with this requirement. Such a person is liable on summary conviction to a fine not exceeding level 4 on the standard scale (currently £2,500).

7.4. Duty Four: To Disclose an Offence After Grant of a Personal Licence

Where a personal licence holder is convicted of a relevant or foreign offence, the Licensing Authority may revoke the licence after consultation with the police. This may occur if the police believe that the crime prevention objective of the Licensing Act 2003 would be undermined by the continuation of the licence. The police must give a notice of objection to the licence continuing within 14 days of receiving notification of the applicant's conviction.

7.5. Duty Five: to Inform a Magistrates Court of a Personal Licence When Charged with a Relevant Offence

When charged with a relevant offence, a personal licence holder must inform a Magistrates court that they hold a personal licence. Anyone found guilty of not complying with this requirement may be liable on summary conviction for a fine not exceeding level 2 on the standard scale (currently *£500*).

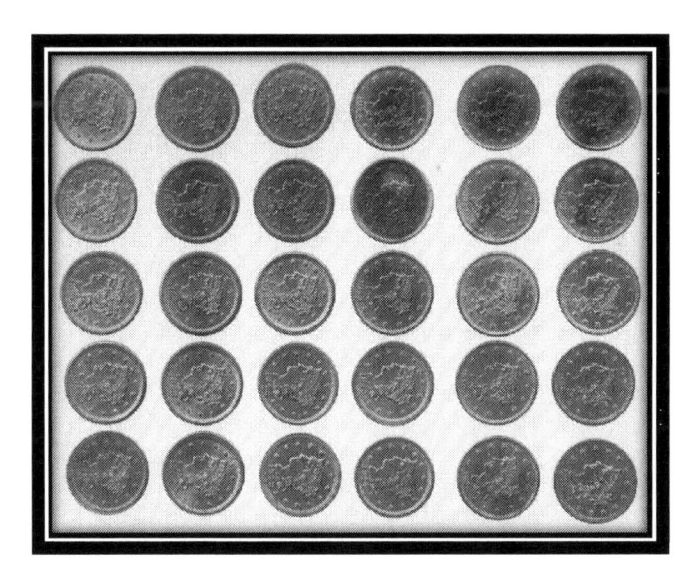

7.6. Reporting a Lost or Stolen Personal Licence

If a personal licence is lost or stolen a duplicate can be obtained from the Licensing Authority that originally issued the licence. This initially required obtaining a lost property number or crime reference number from the local Police and paying a fee to the Licensing Authority.

Following the 2012-2013 Alcohol Strategy Consultation the Government expressed the intention to remove the requirement to report the loss or theft of licences to the police. This measure was enacted 26 May 2015 via the Deregulation Act 2015. Now, if a licence is misplaced the holder simply needs to request a new one from the local Licensing Authority to which they originally applied.

7.7. The 5 Duties of the Personal Licence Holder - Review Questions

See section 20 for answers

1. How many duties does a Licence holder have?

(A) 1

(B) 3

(C) 10

(D) 5

2. Failure to notify the Licensing Authority of a relevant conviction during the application period may result in:

(A) Imprisonment

(B) A fine and/or imprisonment

(C) A fine not exceeding 3 on the standard scale

(D) A fine not in excess of level 4 on the standard scale

3. When must a personal licence holder notify a Licensing Authority of a change to name and/or address?

(A) Within seven days

(B) As soon as is reasonably practicable

(C) Before the end of the month

(D) At any time before the licence expires

4. Where a Court in England and Wales convicts a personal licence holder of a relevant offence, they must:

(A) Issue an immediate penalty fine

(B) Notify the relevant Licensing Authority as soon as possible following judgment

(C) Suspend or revoke the personal licence

(D) Act in accordance with Data Protection provisions

8. THE PREMISES LICENCE

As previously discussed, the Licensing Act 2003 separates the licensing of premises from the licensing of persons. This is a move away from the old system which confused the suitability of the premises with the eligibility of the person applying for a licence.

8.1. What is a Premises Licence?

A premises licence is defined by the Licensing Act 2003 as a licence that authorises the use of specified premises for the carrying on of one or more 'licensable activities'.

8.2. What are Licensable Activities?

As discussed in section 3 of this manual, licensable activities are -

1. ***The sale by retail of alcohol***
2. ***The supply of alcohol*** by or on behalf of a club to, or to the order of, a member of a club
3. ***The provision of regulated entertainment*** *before 8AM or after 11PM*, and
4. ***The provision of late-night refreshment***

8.3. Mandatory Conditions on a Premises Licence

Where a premises licence authorises the sale or supply of alcohol, there are seven mandatory conditions attached to the licence. A "***responsible person***" must ensure compliance with the mandatory conditions. For licensed premises this means the premises licence holder, designated premises supervisor, personal licence holder or person aged over 18 authorised by such a holder or supervisor. In relation to club premises certificates, it means a member or officer of a club who is present and able to prevent a supply of alcohol. The mandatory conditions are as follows:

1. Supplies of alcohol can only be made when a ***Designated Premises Supervisor***, who is a personal licence holder, has been appointed in respect of the premises
2. All sales of alcohol must be made or authorised by ***personal licence holder***. Anyone selling alcohol without a licence must be given permission by a licence holder - preferably written.

NB: Not complying with conditions 1 or 2 would make sales of alcohol an unauthorised licensable activity punishable by an unlimited fine and/or 6 months imprisonment.

3. ***Irresponsible drinks promotions*** must not take place. There is an outright ban on the following types of promotions:

    - Drinking games or other activities that require/encourage the drinking of a quantity of alcohol (or as much as possible) within a time limit. This does not include "drinking up time".
    - Selling or supplying alcohol in association with promotional material condoning, encouraging or glamorising antisocial behaviour and/or drunkenness.
    - Dispensing alcohol directly by one person into the mouth of another (e.g. 'Dentist Chair' games).

    The following promotions are prohibited where there is a "significant risk" to the licensing. If in doubt, advice should be obtained from the licensing authority and/or police.

    - Providing alcohol free or for a fixed or discounted fee
    - Providing free or discounted alcohol or any other thing as a prize to encourage or reward the consumption of alcohol over a period of 24 hours or less.

4. ***Free, drinkable tap water*** should be provided on request where reasonably available.

5. Alcohol must be available for purchase in the following *small measures (which customers must be made aware of)*:

   - Beer/cider: 1/2 pints
   - Gin, rum, vodka, whisky: 25ml or 35ml shots
   - Wine: by the glass in 125ml glasses (except sparkling).

   The Licensing Act 2003 (Mandatory Licensing Conditions) (Amendment) Order 2014 requires that measures must be displayed in a menu, price list, or other printed material. Where a customer doesn't specify a measure, they must be made aware of the range of measures available, either verbally or by ensuring that they have seen the printed material. This process does not need to be repeated as long as the customer continues to be aware of the measures available.

6. Every premises selling alcohol must have an *age verification policy* requiring staff to check the ID of anyone who appears to be under 18 years of age (or any such older age as may be specified in the policy). The designated premises supervisor in relation to the premises licence must ensure that the supply of alcohol at the premises is carried on in accordance with the age verification policy. The policy must require individuals who appear to the responsible person to be under 18 years of age (or such older age as may be specified in the policy) to produce on request, before being served alcohol, identification bearing their photograph, date of birth and either (a) a holographic mark, or (b) an ultraviolet feature.

7. There is a ban on the *sale of alcohol below the "permitted price"* (the level of alcohol duty plus VAT). For example, as at May 2014, a can of average strength lager could not be sold for less than £0.39 and a standard bottle of vodka could not be sold for less than £8.72.

   If the relevant "responsible person" does not have the remit to adjust pricing, responsibility is applicable to the company headquarters and the person/persons who can enact such changes.

NB: Non-compliance with condition 7 is punishable by an unlimited fine and/or 6 months imprisonment.

8.4. The Designated Premises Supervisor (DPS)

A premises can only sell or supply alcohol if a Designated Premises Supervisor (DPS) has been appointed, and is named on the premises licence. The DPS must be a personal licence holder and in day-to-day control of the premises (although he or she can manage more than one licensed premises at any given time).

8.5. The Responsibilities of the Designated Premises Supervisor (DPS)

The DPS provides a single point of accountability in licensed premises. ***There can hence only be one DPS*** per premises

- A nominated DPS must consent to the position in writing. A copy of this must be sent to the Licensing Authority. The police may object to a particular DPS if they believe that the appointment would undermine the crime and prevention objective
- The premises licence holder can also be the DPS
- The personal licence holder who actually authorises sale of alcohol does not have to be the DPS
- The DPS should promote the licensing objectives and discourage drink driving by:
  - Liaising with taxi and cab firms and displaying their phone numbers. In some cases, taxi firms may be prepared to install a direct line for cabs to be ordered
  - Displaying bus timetable information and finding out whether local bus firms run late-night services
  - Providing a club or pub bus for customers
  - Avoiding anti-drink-driving gimmicks, such as breath-testing machines and patented medicines that claim to hasten the sobering-up process
  - Following the 2012-2013 Alcohol Strategy Consultation the Government has made the DPS responsible for the management and implementation of the premises age verification policy.

8.6. What is an Operating Schedule?

An operating schedule sets out various details on how the premises is proposed to operate when carrying on licensable activities. Completing an Operating Schedule is part of the premises licence application process.

If the premises licence is granted the operating schedule will be incorporated into the licence itself and will set out the permitted activities and the limitations on them.

8.6.1. What should an Operating Schedule include?

- Opening hours and times during which licensable activities will take place. These are subject to objections from interested parties such as local residents, or authorities such as the police, being upheld.

- The type of premises (public house, off licence etc.) and the facilities available to customers (e.g. beer garden).

- What licensable activities will be offered on the premises. This should include details of any public entertainment and late-night refreshment to be provided.

- If alcohol is to be sold the name of the DPS must be included as well as whether the alcohol is for consumption on or off the premises.

- The operating schedule must show how the business will promote the Four Licensing Objectives stated in the 2003 Act. Refer to Sections 15-18 for further information.

8.6.2. Late Night Opening, the Late Night Levy and EMROs

Under the Licensing Act 2003, ***permitted opening hours are theoretically continuous***. It is therefore possible for a premises licence to allow 24-hour opening. Most licensed premises do not go this far although it is now not unusual for pubs to stay open all night during the weekend in urban areas. There is no obligation for the premises licence holder to stay open until the closure time specified on the licence, but licensable activities must cease once the closure time has been reached.

24-hour licensing has arguably exacerbated social, health and crime-related issues in some areas. Because of this two new measures were introduced in October 2012 by the Police Reform and Social Responsibility Act 2011. These were the *Late Night Levy* and *Early Morning Restriction Orders (EMROs)*. Both measures are effectively discretionary mechanisms, open to use by Licensing Authorities, to deal with the problems of late night drinking.

The late night levy provides Licensing Authorities with the *discretionary power to raise monies from late opening alcohol retailers* with the contribution being used to help police the late night economy. The Licensing Authority can retain up to 30% of the net levy to fund non-policing activities such as taxi marshals, late night town wardens and street cleaning services.

The levy, if implemented, applies to premises selling alcohol between 12am and 6am. It is up to the Licensing Authority to determine the relevant hours within that period, to be known as the 'late night supply period'. The levy is payable by on-licensed and off-licensed premises (but will **NOT** include premises covered by a Temporary Event Notice (TEN - see section 10). If a Licensing Authority decides to implement the levy they will need to consult with the Police and affected premises *for a period lasting for at least 12 weeks.*

The Late Night Levy has not, however, been widely implemented and has been subject to criticism. Section 142 and Schedule 18 of the Policing and Crime Act 2017 aimed to make the levy more flexible, allowing authorities to introduce the levy in specific areas rather than across the whole of the local authority. Licensing authorities are now required to publish information on how the funds raised by the levy are spent.

A key change in the Policing and Crime Act 2017 is that the levy will extend to premises that are permitted to offer late night refreshment, for example takeaways. Premises only serving hot, non-alcoholic drinks are excluded.

Under the Policing and Crime Act 2017, Police and Crime Commissioners now have a statutory right to request that consideration is given by a licensing authority to implementing a Late Night Levy in their area. Such a request must be then given consideration by the licensing authority and the response to the request must be published. This published response must include reasons, including an explanation of the outcome of the authority's considerations.

The EMRO empowers Licensing Authorities to restrict alcohol sales in the whole or part of their areas **between midnight and 6am**. The Licensing Authority has the discretion to decide which days the EMRO will apply on and in which areas it will apply. Theoretically the authorities may choose to implement EMROs for the city/town centre or for identified problem areas. EMROs will apply to Temporary Event Notices as well as permanent licences. Implementation of an EMRO requires a **28 week consultation period**.

8.7. The Premises Licence Application Procedure

8.7.1. Who can apply for a premises licence?

To apply for a premises licence an individual must be over 18. For applications from individuals, or partnerships which are not limited liability partnerships, proof of the right to live and work in the UK is required.

In the example case of an off-licence the applicant may be either the business owner or the premises owner (who lets out the premises for business purposes). If the premises owner applies for the licence they will generally arrange a contractual agreement with the business owner. This also applies to most leased public houses. With company-run supermarkets however, it is always the holding company, not the manager, who applies for the licence. The same applies to company-run pub chains.

8.7.2. The application procedure

As with the personal licence application, the form of application for a premises licence is prescribed. Applications are made to the authority in which the premises is located. The application must include:

- For individual applicants, or for partnerships which are not limited liability partnerships, proof of the right to live and work in the UK.

- The fee (set by central Government). Note that an **annual fee**, also set by central Government, will also be payable after grant of the licence. Following implementation of the Police Reform and Social Responsibility Act 2011, **non-payment of the annual fee** is now a valid reason for suspension of premises licences and club premises certificates. **A 21 day 'grace period'** after the annual fee becomes due is allowed for payment of an overdue fee.

- Plans of the premises in scale (1cm to 100cm, unless otherwise agreed by the Authority)

- Consent forms signed by the Designated Premises Supervisor

- The completed application forms and the operating schedule

8.7.3. Publicity of premises licence application - *the 28 day publicity rule*

You must display notice of a premises licence application in at least one place at, or on the site of, the premises. This should be done for **at least 28 days** - starting the day following the application is made to the Licensing Authority. The notice must be a pale blue colour, at least A4 size and in black type. It must be displayed in a place where it can conveniently be seen

8.7.4. Publicity of premises licence application in a local newspaper

In addition to the 28 day publicity rule, a notice must also be published in a local newspaper. This must be done at least once **within 10 working days**, starting the day after the application is given to the Licensing Authority. A copy of this advertisement may need to be sent to the Licensing Authority.

8.7.5. Notification of Responsible Authorities

The applicant must also notify 'Responsible Authorities' of their application (see section 5.9.2). These include the Police, the Fire Service, the Health and Safety Agency, the Local Authority Director of Public Health, the Environmental Health Department, the Planning Department, the Social Services department and the Local Licensing Authority.

8.7.6. Representations by Responsible Authorities or the general public

A representation is essentially an objection to the grant of all, or part, of the licence. All representations must be about the expected consequences of granting the licence on the promotion of at least one of the four licensing objectives (see sections 15-18).

For example, if it was felt that insufficient measures were in place to prevent your customers from disturbing local residents, then a responsible authority, or member of the public potentially affected by grant of the licence, could make a representation. Representations must be made *within 28 days* of receipt of your application.

If there are valid representations received within the consultation period then a hearing must be convened within a *further 28 day period* in order that the Licensing Committee of the Licensing Authority can determine the outcome of the application (see section 19).

8.8. Obtaining Advance Consent for a Premises Licence Where the Premises are Under Construction/Alteration - the Provisional Statement

A 'provisional statement' is an application made on behalf of someone who is either constructing new licensed premises or substantially altering existing premises. It enables the applicant to obtain confirmation that a premises licence will be granted for the purpose of carrying on licensable activities once the building or substantial alteration is completed.

8.9. What Happens When a Premises Licence Holder Dies, Becomes Insolvent or Incapacitated? - the Interim Authority Notice

A premises licence terminates upon the death, incapacity or insolvency of the premises licence holder. In order to ensure continuity of the business, an interim authority may be sought by anyone with a prescribed interest in the premises - such as the freeholder or someone connected with the former premises licence holder. This authority lasts for a maximum of *two months*.

8.9.1. Interim authority notice procedure

An interim authority notice must be given to the Licensing Authority within seven days of the premises licence lapsing. The application must be copied to the police who may, within 48 hours, object if they think the crime prevention objective would be undermined.

The business may operate as soon as the notice is served on the Licensing Authority, but not before.

8.10. Premises Licence Reviews

If problems arise at a licensed premises, such as antisocial or criminal behaviour, a licence review may result. An application for a review of a premises licence can be made by a responsible authority such as the police, or any member of the public affected by the premises licence.

Licence reviews are carried out by the local Licensing Authority. On determination of a review, the following actions may be taken:

- *Revocation of the licence*
- *Suspension of the licence for up to 3 months*
- *Exclusion of a licensable activity from the licence*
- *Modification of licence conditions*
- *Removal of a Designated Premises Supervisor*

8.10.1. Expedited/Summary Reviews

In cases of serious crime/disorder a police officer of rank Superintendent or above may request a summary review of a premises licence. This is done by signature of a certificate followed by submission to the local Licensing Authority.

The Licensing Authority must **carry out an interim review within 48 hours of receipt of the certificate** determining whether, and what, interim steps are necessary to promote the licensing objectives. **The premises licence holder does not need to be made aware of this interim review.** Actions taken by the Licensing Authority **may include licence suspension** (effectively closing the premises).

If the premises licence holder is not present at the interim review, they may appeal any decisions made. The Licensing Authority **must consider this appeal within 48 hours**. They may then, subject to the licensing objectives, modify any interim measures imposed.

A full review must then take place **within 28 days** of the initial request and is carried out as per a normal review.

Section 136 of the Policing and Crime Act 2017 put in place a restriction so that licence holders are only able to make further representations after their initial representations have been considered, if there has been a material change in circumstances since the consideration hearing.

Section 137 of the Policing and Crime Act 2017 amended the Licensing Act 2003 so as to require the licensing authority to determine at the review hearing what interim steps should be in place pending the outcome of any appeal, or the expiry of the time limit for making an appeal. These arrangements allow licensing authorities and the police to take effective enforcement action, and are fairer for businesses. Licensees and the police will be able to appeal the interim steps to a magistrates' court.

8.11. Premises Licence Review Questions

See section 20 for answers

1. What is a premises licence under the Licensing Act 2003?

(A) A Licence permitting a retailer to set up retail premises

(B) A Licence authorising premises to be used for one or more licensable activities

(C) A Licence permitting the sale of luxury goods throughout the UK

(D) A Licence to carry out non-licensable activities

2. Which of the following would be a major variation to a premises licence?

(A) A change to the designed premises supervisor

(B) A change to the premises' licence holder

(C) A change to the opening hours

(D) A temporary activity

3. How many mandatory conditions may be attached to a premises' licence where alcohol sales are permitted?

(A) One

(B) Seven

(C) None

(D) Five

4. What does 'DPS' stand for?

(A) Director of Protection of Standards

(B) Designated Personal Supervisor

(C) Designer of Property Services

(D) Designated Premises Supervisor

5. What are the requirements for an individual to become a DPS?

(A) The individual must have be over the age of 25

(B) The individual must hold a personal licence

(C) The individual must be the retail owner of the premises

(D) The individual cannot have a criminal record

6. What is an operating schedule?

(A) The time that the retail premises usually close

(B) The time that the retail premises usually opens

(C) The recruitment of staff policy in the licensed premises

(D) The details stating how the premises operates when carrying on licensable activities

9. The Club Premises Certificate

A 'club' means premises such as a Conservative Club or a social club where the alcohol is owned by the members. Technically therefore, the alcohol is not sold, but supplied to members.

Under the old regime, non-profit making private clubs such as Labour and Conservative clubs and working men's clubs could supply alcohol to children. This is now a serious offence.

9.1. Qualifying Club Criteria

A club premises certificate is only for use by qualifying clubs. A number of criteria must be met to be considered a qualifying club. These are:

- That under the rules of the club, persons may not be admitted to membership, or to any of the privileges of membership, before an interval of at least two days has passed

- That the club is established and conducted in good faith as a club

- That the club has at least 25 members

- That alcohol is not supplied to members on the premises otherwise than by, or on behalf of, the club

To qualify as a club authorised to supply alcohol to its members and guests, additional conditions must be met. These are:

- The purchase and supply of alcohol is managed by a committee made up of elected members of the club all aged over 18 years
- No person may receive any commission, percentage or similar payment at the expense of the club for purchases of alcohol by the club
- No person may receive any monetary benefit from the supply of alcohol to members or guests apart from to benefit the club as a whole

9.2. Qualifying Club Activities - What Are They?

The three qualifying 'Club Activities' carried out on behalf of, or to the order of, a club are:

1. Supplying alcohol to a member of the club
2. The sale by retail of alcohol to a guest of a member of the club, for consumption on the premises where the sale takes place, and
3. The provision of regulated entertainment to members of the club and their guests.

9.3. What Are The Benefits of Holding a Club Premises Certificate?

- There is no requirement to hold a personal licence.
- There is no requirement to specify a Designated Premises Supervisor
- There are significant cost savings involved
- More relaxed police and magistrates closure orders

Nevertheless, instant club membership is not permitted and members must wait at least **two days** between their application and admission to the club.

9.4. Applying for a Club Premises Certificate

As with the personal and premises licence application, the form of application for a club premises certificate is prescribed. Application forms may be obtained from the applicant's local council. The application must be accompanied by:

- The fee
- Plans of the premises (in the prescribed format)
- The club rules
- A club operating schedule

9.4.1. The club operating schedule

A "club operating schedule" is a document which is in the prescribed form, and includes a statement of the following:

- The qualifying club activities to which the application relates ("the relevant qualifying club activities"),
- The times during which it is proposed that the relevant qualifying club activities are to take place,
- Any other times during which it is proposed that the premises are to be open to members and their guests,
- Where the relevant qualifying club activities include the supply of alcohol, whether the supplies are proposed to be for consumption on the premises or both on and off the premises, and
- The steps which it is proposed to take to promote the licensing objectives (see sections 15-18).

9.4.2. Advertising the application and notifying Responsible Authorities

The requirements for advertising the application and notifying responsible authorities are very similar to those for premises licence applications (see section 8.7). Responsible authorities (such as the police) have **28 days** within which to make an objection.

The Licensing Authority must determine new and variation applications within **two months**. If they fail to do so, and no objections have been raised by the police, the application is treated as granted.

9.4.3. Certificate duration and annual fees

Once granted, a club premises certificate has **no time limit** and will continue to have effect unless it is withdrawn by the Licensing Authority, following an application for the review of the certificate, or if the club ceases to be a qualifying club or surrenders the certificate.

Once a club certificate has been granted the Regulations may require payment of an annual fee to the relevant Licensing Authority.

9.5. Clubs and Right of Entry

9.5.1. Inspection of a premises before grant of certificate

For premises licence applications a police officer or authorised person (fire officer, officer of the Licensing Authority, health and safety officer or environmental health officer) may, at any reasonable time, enter a premises subject to a licensing application to assess the effect of the application on the licensing objectives. However, in the case of Club Premises Certificates, **48 hours notice** must be given before inspection can take place.

9.5.2. Other powers of entry and search

Where a club premises certificate is already in place, a police constable may enter and search a premises if he or she believes drug dealing may be taking place, or a breach of the peace is likely.

9.6. The Club Certificate Review Questions

See section 20 for answers

1. In what circumstances may a retail sale take place in a qualifying club?

(A) Sale of alcohol to the guest of a member

(B) Sale of alcohol cannot take place in the qualifying club

(C) Sale of alcohol to a member

(D) Sale of alcohol to a committee member

2. When do Authorised Persons have no immediate right of entry to Licensed Premises?

(A) Where the Licensed Premises has supervisors on the entry to the premises

(B) Where the Licensed Premises is not within a one mile radius of a town centre

(C) Where the Licensed Premises only has a Club Premises Certificate in force

(D) Authorised Persons have a right to entry at all times

3. How long does a chief officer of police have to object to a Club Premises Certificate?

(A) Up to 28 days from receipt of the application

(B) Up to 14 days from receipt of the application

(C) Up to three months from receipt of the application

(D) Up to six months from receipt of the application

4. What happens where a Licensing Authority fails to determine an application for a Club Premises Certificate within 2 months:

(A) The retailer may apply to the Magistrates Court

(B) The Licensing Authority is required to pay a fine to the retailer

(C) The application is to be treated as granted unless a timely objection has been received from the chief of police

(D) The retailer should chase the Licensing Authority persistently

5. How long does a Club Premises Certificate last?

(A) Indefinitely unless it is withdrawn or surrendered

(B) It needs to be renewed every six months

(C) 5 years

(D) 10 years

6. Where a Club Premises Certificate has been issued, the Regulations may require:

(A) That Licensing Authorities gain access to the club free of charge for social events

(B) The payment of an annual fee to the relevant Licensing Authority

(C) That the Certificate holders attend regular training events

(D) The Premises to be open to all members of the public

10. THE TEMPORARY EVENTS NOTICE ('TEN')

Part 5 of the Licensing Act 2003 as modified by the Police Reform and Social Responsibility Act 2011 enables individuals - 'premises users' - to carry out licensable activities on a temporary basis. This provision is subject to various conditions and limits relating to the number of events that may be permitted. ***Individuals must be at least 18 years old to apply.***

Individuals can obtain a temporary licence by means of a Temporary Events Notice (or 'TEN'). There are two types of TEN:

1. **The *'standard'* TEN** - must be served on the Licensing Authority and responsible authorities at least ***10 working days*** before the first day of the event.

2. **The *'late'* TEN** - may be submitted ***between 9 and 5 working days*** before the first day of the event. However, if objections are received to a late TEN application, the event will not be permitted to go ahead and there will not be any right of appeal against this decision

10. The Temporary Events Notice ('TEN')

Different limits apply depending on whether or not the person carrying out licensable activities holds a personal licence and how frequently they intend to use the premises.

- Personal licence holders can apply for up to **50 TENs a year** (with no more than **10 late TENs**)
- Persons without a personal licence can apply for up to **5 TENs a year** (with no more than **2 late TENs**)
- A TEN can only be sought where **499 or less people** are attending the event
- A premises may be used for temporary events on no more than **15 occasions** (this was increased from 12 from **1 January 2016** as legislated for by the Deregulation Act 2015), stretching over an overall **maximum of 21 days** in any one calendar year.
- Each event is limited to **7 days** ("not exceeding **168 hours**") and a minimum of 24 hours must elapse between any two events

10.1. In What Circumstances Would a 'TEN' be Required?

10.1.1. The personal licence holder and TEN's

A TEN is useful where a personal licence holder wishes to carry out one or more licensable activities at premises not covered by a premises licence relating to those activities.

All of the following activities are licensable, and as such will require submission of a TEN:

- **Sale and supply of alcohol**
- **Regulated late night refreshment (hot food & drinks between 11pm and 5am)**
- **Regulated entertainment <u>occurring before 8am or after 11pm</u>:**
    - Plays
    - Films
    - Indoor sporting events
    - Boxing or wrestling (with certain exemptions)
    - Live music
    - Recorded Music

- Anything of a similar description
- Provision of facilities for such activities

One example requiring a TEN would be where a publican is asked to run a temporary bar for a wedding at a venue not licensed for the sale of alcohol. Another would be where a bar or restaurant is licensed to sell alcohol but not to provide late-night music events to its customers.

10.1.2. The non-personal licence holder and TEN's

A TEN is useful where an individual who does not hold a personal licence wishes to carry out one or more licensable activities at any premises (whether or not they are covered by a premises licence relating to those activities). An example would be where an individual wishes to run a bar and provide a band at a 50th wedding anniversary party. This may be done by the same person on no more than five occasions in any one calendar year.

10.2. How is a Temporary Activity Defined

A permitted Temporary Activity is defined as one that is carried on in accordance with a Temporary Event Notice to the relevant Licensing Authority and which satisfies the following conditions:

- The Temporary Event Notice has been duly acknowledged by the Licensing Authority and the police have been notified,
- The Temporary Event Notice has not been subsequently withdrawn by the individual giving the notice, and

10. The Temporary Events Notice ('TEN')

- The Licensing Authority has not issued a counter-notice. A counter notice would be issued following a hearing of any police objections. Objections may be raised if the police believe the event could undermine the crime prevention objective (section 15).

10.3. Temporary Events Notice (TEN) Applications

An individual, known as a 'premises user', must prepare the TEN application setting out certain details about the proposed event such as:

- The *licensable activities that are to be carried out*,
- The *total length of the event* - which must not exceed *168 hours*,
- *The times* during the event that the licensable activities are to be carried out (e.g. where an individual wishes to organise an event that covers 36 hours and where the bar will be open for two evenings within that time),
- The *maximum number of people* to be allowed on to the premises at any one time - which must be equal to, or less than *499*,
- *Whether any alcohol sales are to be made for consumption on or off the premises* (or both), and
- Any other information that may be prescribed by regulations

Two copies of the TEN must be served on the Licensing Authority no later than:

- *'Standard' TENs - 10 working days* before the start of the event (not including the day of the event).
- *'Late TENs' - between 9 and 5 working days* before the start of the event

These copies must be accompanied by the prescribed fee. Although 10 days is the minimum period specified for standard TENs, it is anticipated that in most circumstances greater notice will be given.

A copy of the TEN must also be served on the *Police and Environmental Health Authorities* within the same time limits before the start of the event. These authorities have the power to object to the TENs. To object they must give an objection notice *within 3 working days* to both the Licensing Authority and the applicant.

10.3.1. Objections to TENs and the issuing of Counter Notices

In the case of a 'standard TEN', if the Police or Environmental Health Authority objects, *the Licensing Authority* must hold a hearing to consider the objection notice, unless the premises user, the police and the licensing section all agree that a hearing is not necessary.

If the Licensing Authority accepts the police objection it must issue a 'counter-notice' to the premises user in which case the event cannot proceed. If the authority does not accept the objection it must inform the relevant responsible authority.

Any decision by the Licensing Authority must be issued to the premises user *at least 24 hours* before the specified event. A failure to do so will result in the premises user being able to proceed with the event.

In the case of a 'late TEN' if an objection is received a counter notice prohibiting the event will be served and *the event will not go ahead*.

10.3.2. Modifying a TENs

The Police and Environmental Health Authority may modify the TEN with the consent of the premises user. In such a case an objection notice will be deemed to have been withdrawn.

The Licensing Authority may also issue a counter notice if the permitted limits have been exceeded.

Before the time of the event the Licensing Authority must acknowledge the notice. The police must consider the notice and decide whether to give notice of objection and if the police object, the Licensing Authority must, if necessary, convene a hearing to decide whether to issue a counter notice.

10.4. The Community and Ancillary Sellers Notice (CAN)

Following the Deregulation Act 2015, the Government made plans to introduce secondary legislation to make it easier for:

- *Ancillary sellers* who wished to sell small amounts of alcohol as an adjunct to their normal business (such as a hairdresser offering a glass of wine with a haircut)
- *Local community groups* who wished to sell alcohol as part of an event.

The new *Community and Ancillary Sellers Notice (CAN)* was intended to operate without a complex application process or licensing hearings. CAN users would be able to simply notify their licensing authority, subject to payment of a small fee, that they would be selling small amounts of alcohol in low risk environments over the course of a year.

As with TENs, licensing authorities, the police and environmental health authorities would have had the power to reject CANs based on the licensing objectives.

It should be noted, however, CANs will not be introduced until such time as Section 67 of the Deregulation Act 2015 is brought into force. Currently no date is proposed for implementation and the House of Lords Select Committee on the Licensing Act 2003 has recommended that Section 67 be repealed (without suggesting a replacement).

10.5. TEN Review Questions

See section 20 for answers

1. What is a 'TEN'?

(A) A Tender Entertainment Notice

(B) A Typical Event Notice

(C) A Temporary Event Notice

(D) A Temporary Entertainment Notice

2. A personal licence holder planning a temporary evening must give notice to:

(A) The Licensing Authority that issued the premises authority

(B) The Licensing Authority that issued the premises licence

(C) Any Licensing Authority in England & Wales

(D) The Licensing Authority where the event is to be held

3. What is the minimum notice required for a 'standard' TENs?

(A) Ten days

(B) Twenty-one days

(C) Twenty four hours

(D) Fourteen days

4. What is the maximum time period of a 'temporary event'?

(A) A period of time not exceeding 96 hours

(B) A period of time not exceeding 12 hours

(C) A period of time not exceeding 15 hours

(D) A period of time not exceeding 168 hours

10. The Temporary Events Notice ('TEN')

5. An individual who does NOT hold a personal licence may carry out temporary activities up to:

(A) 5 times in a calendar year (with no more than 2 late TENs)

(B) 5 times in a calendar year (with no more than 3 late TENs)

(C) 12 times in a calendar year

(D) 15 times a year in a calendar year

11. SUSPENSION AND CLOSURE - POLICE POWERS

11.1. Police Power to Close all Premises in an Area Experiencing Disorder

Section 160 of the Licensing Act 2003 sets out the police power to close *all premises subject to premises licence*, or a Temporary Event Notice, that are located in a particular geographical area for a period up to **24 hours**.

Only a police office of the rank of *superintendent* or above can apply to the magistrates' court to request this type of closure.

The court may not make such an order unless it is satisfied that it is necessary to prevent disorder.

A constable may use necessary force to close any premises covered by such an order. It is an offence to keep premises open if they are subject to a closure order.

Such orders should normally be sought where the police anticipate public order problems (very often fuelled by the ready availability of alcohol) as a result of intelligence or publicly available information, but may also be used in an emergency.

Events which might justify action under Section 160 could include football fixtures with a history of public order problems and demonstrations which are thought likely to be hijacked by extreme or violent groups. Where it is possible to anticipate disorder in this way, the courts should be involved and make the decision on the application of a police officer of the rank of superintendent or above as to whether widespread closure is justified.

11.2. Police Closure Order for Specified Premises

Section 161 of the Licensing Act 2003 empowers a senior police officer (***inspector*** or above) to immediately close a ***specific premises for up to 24 hours***. Such a closure order may be made on two grounds:

1. Where there is ***actual or likely disorder*** to the extent that the closure of the related premises is necessary for public safety, or

2. Where the closure is necessary to prevent a ***public nuisance***, owing to noise emanating from the premises.

These immediate closure orders should only be used to counter immediate and unexpected risks. Police should not use such closure orders where it has been possible to anticipate the disorder arising. Following such a closure order, the premises will be subject to a ***licence review within 28 days***. If the premises close voluntarily however, this review may not necessarily follow.

11.3. Conduct of the Premises Licence Holder

Section 161 of the Licensing Act 2003 also provides that the senior police officer must consider the conduct of the premises licence holder, manager, Designated Premises Supervisor or premises user who has given a Temporary Event Notice, before making a closure order. If they have acted incompetently, inadequately or actually provoked or caused the problems or, alternatively, have called the police in promptly and acted sensibly to try to prevent disorder or noise nuisance, the officer may take these factors into account.

11.4. Extension and Cancellation of Closure Orders

In limited circumstances, Section 162 of the Licensing Act 2003 allows a senior police officer to extend the period for which a closure order may have effect. Such an extension may be for a **further period of 24 hours**. More than one extension may be made.

Section 163 of the Licensing Act 2003 also enables a senior police officer to cancel a closure order **at any time** before it has been considered by a ***magistrates' court***. Referral to the magistrates' court for consideration is mandatory under the new regime (Section 164 of the Licensing Act 2003). Such a cancellation must be made where the officer no longer believes that closure of the premises is necessary because of reductions in the risk of disorder, or likely disorder or noise emanating from the premises.

The officer must give notice to the licence holder, Designated Premises Supervisor, premises user or manager of the premises where it is decided to cancel a closure order.

11.5. Application to the Magistrates' Court by Police

After a closure order comes into effect, Section 164 of the Licensing Act 2003 requires the responsible senior police officer to apply to the magistrates' court without delay to allow for the consideration of the order by the court.

Notice of such an application and details of the order itself must also be given to the relevant Licensing Authority.

11.6. Consideration of Closure Orders by the Magistrates' Court

The relevant magistrates' court must hold a hearing to consider the closure order (Section 165 of the Licensing Act 2003). The court can take a number of courses of action in relation to the order, including revoking the closure order, or ordering an extension of it pending a review of the order by the Licensing Authority.

The court may also make an order determining that the premises should be, or should remain closed until such a review has been completed.

11.7. Appeals Against the Decision of the Magistrates' Court

There is a right of appeal to the Crown Court against decisions made by a magistrates' court (Section 166 of the Licensing Act 2003).

To claim damages against police following a closure order, a claimant must prove that the police acted in bad faith or in contravention of the Human Rights Act 1998.

11.8. Review of a Premises Licence Following a Closure Order

Section 167 of the Licensing Act 2003 requires the Licensing Authority to review the premises licence of any premises subject to a closure order confirmed by a magistrates' court within **28 days**. The Licensing Authority may take steps to further the licensing objectives, including the suspension of the licence for up to **3 months**, revocation of the licence, modification of the licence conditions, exclusion of certain licensable activities or the removal of the Designated Premises Supervisor.

For example, where the Licensing Authority determines that the inexperience of the Designated Premises Supervisor has contributed to the level of disorder leading to the closure order, it may specify removal of that individual. Similarly, it may determine that additional security staff should be employed to further reduce disorder.

11.9. Extended Closure Powers: Anti-Social Behaviour Act 2003

Police also have a power available under the Anti-Social Behaviour Act 2003 to close premises where there is the production, supply or use of *class A drugs* and serious nuisance or disorder. This power provides an extra tool to the police to enable rapid action against a premises where there is a Class A drug problem, enabling its closure in as little as *48 hours* should this be necessary.

11.10. Extended Closure Powers: Violent Crime Reduction Act 2006

On 6 April 2007, the Violent Crime Reduction Act 2006 amended Part 8 of the Licensing Act 2003 to insert a *new offence of persistently selling alcohol to children*. This requires alcohol to be sold to a minor on *2 or more occasions in 3 consecutive months*. The offence carries a penalty of an *unlimited fine*, possible loss of licence and closure.

Where a premises licence holder is found guilty of persistently selling alcohol to children a *voluntary closure of between 48 and 336 hours* may be agreed with police/Trading Standards as an alternative to prosecution.

11.11. Suspension and Closure - Police Powers Review Questions

See section 20 for answers

1. Specified licensed premises may be closed by a police officer of which rank?

(A) Superintendent or above

(B) Sergeant or above

(C) Any police officer

(D) Inspector or above

2. What may the Licensing Authority do if a Closure Order is made against a specific premises?

(A) Renew the retailers Personal License

(B) Suspend the licence indefinitely

(C) Suspend the licence for up to three months or revoke the licence

(D) Send the retailer on licensing courses as well as suspending the licence for up to three months

3. A police power under the Anti-Social Behaviour Act 2003 has:

(A) The power to not allow a person with a conviction on licensed premises

(B) The power to close premises for any reason they think fit

(C) The power to close premises where Class A drugs are used

(D) The power to allow the premises to serve a person who appears drunk

4. A senior police officer may cancel a Closure Order

(A) At any time

(B) Only during the premises opening hours

(C) After 24 hours

(D) After 6 months

5. The police can close specific licensed premises due to noise problems or public safety without a court order for a period of up to:

(A) 6 hours maximum

(B) 24 hour maximum

(C) 72 hour maximum

(D) To the end of licensing hours that day

6. To claim damages against police following a closure order, a claimant must prove:

(A) The constable made a mistake in his actions in performing his duties

(B) To police had taken so long to attend, a closure order was the only option

(C) The police acted in bad faith or in contravention of the Human Rights Act 1998

(D) The police issued a closure order only because of lack of police numbers

12. Closure Powers - The Local Authority

Part 7 of the Anti-Social Behaviour Act 2003 gives the chief executive officer of the relevant local authority the power to make a Closure Order in relation to a premises.

There appears to be a strong link between late licences and the number of Closure Orders made by local authorities concerned over noise levels.

12.1. Closure by the Local Authority

A Closure Order can only be made in circumstances where:

(a) A public nuisance is being caused by noise coming from premises, and

(b) The closure of the premises is necessary to prevent a nuisance

This power applies to premises which have a premises licence or which are operating under the authority of a Temporary Event Notice. The Order can require premises to be kept closed for up to **24 hours** and begins either when the manager of the premises receives written notice of the order or when it is affixed to the licensed premises.

12. Closure Powers - The Local Authority

A person commits an offence if he permits premises to be open in contravention of a closure order. If found guilty of such a offence may be liable upon summary conviction to a term of imprisonment not exceeding *three months*, or a fine not exceeding *£20.000*, or both.

Once a Closure Order is in force, a review of the premises licence is automatically undertaken by the Licensing Authority.

12.2. Delegation of Closure Powers to Environmental Health Officers (EHO)

The chief executive officer of a local authority may authorise an Environmental Health Officer to exercise a power or duty of the chief executive officer in order to:

- Investigate complaints of noise-nuisance at night.
- Issue a Closure Order to prevent noise-nuisance from licensed premises.

The power enabling Environmental Health Officers to close licensed premises where a public nuisance is being caused by noise is provided under the ***Anti-Social Behaviour Act 2003***. In these circumstances, a review of the premises licence is not an automatic result.

The Environmental Officer must give the manager of the premises written notice of the closure order. The maximum penalty for failing to comply with such a closure order is *three months* imprisonment, *£20,000 fine* or both.

12.3. Closure Powers - The Local Authority Review Questions

See section 20 for answers

1. What must the Environmental Officer do before the premises can be closed?

(A) Local residents must be informed that the premises is due for closure

(B) The Environmental Officer must give the manager of the premises written notice of the closure order

(C) The Environmental Officer must contact the police to close the premises

(D) The retailer must be informed by telephone that the premises must be closed

2. What is the maximum penalty for failing to close when instructed to do so by an Environmental Health Officer?

(A) Six months' imprisonment

(B) Six months' imprisonment, a fine or both

(C) Three months' imprisonment and/or an unlimited fine

(D) £20,000 fine

3. What Act empowers the Environmental Health Officer (EHO) to close noisy premises in order to prevent nuisance?

(A) The Environmental Health Act 2007

(B) The Antisocial Behaviour Act 2003

(C) The Licensing Act 2003

(D) The Supply of Alcohol Act 1995

4. In what circumstances is a closure notice on licensed premises deemed served under the Licensing Act 2003?

(A) Where the Closure Notice has been affixed to a tree outside the licensed premises

(B) Where the Closure Notice has been sent in first-class post

(C) Where the Closure Notice is affixed to the licensed premises

(D) Where a police officer has read the contents of the Closure Notice to the retailer over the telephone

5. What must the Licensing Authority undertake where a local authority Closure Order has come into force?

(A) The despatch of an immediate fine

(B) The immediate suspension of the personal licences attached to the premises

(C) A review of the premises licence

(D) The Licensing Authority is at liberty to decide what to do next

13. RIGHT OF ENTRY TO LICENSED PREMISES

13.1. Who has the Right of Entry to Licensed Premises and When?

Authorised persons listed below all have rights of entry at all reasonable times for the purposes of carrying out their statutory duties.

- *Police officers*
- *Trading standards officers*
- *Environmental health officers*
- *Fire Service*
- *Building control, and council licensing officers*
- *Customs and Excise officers*

A constable or other authorised person has a right to enter premises at all reasonable times whilst an application for a premises licence is pending, in order to consider whether or not to make an objection to the Licensing Authority. At all other times constables can rely on the offence under the Police Act 1996, section 89, of obstructing a constable in the execution of his duty.

13. Right of Entry to Licensed Premises

Specifically police officers and other authorised persons have the following rights of entry and inspection:

- A police officer or other **authorised person** (local authority officer, health and safety or fire officer) **may, at any reasonable time, enter the premises** to which any application or notice for a grant, variation or review of a premises licence has been made, in order to assess its effect on the licensing objectives. **In the case of club premises certificates, 48 hours notice** must be given.

- A police officer or other authorised person may at any time enter any premises if they have reason to believe that they are used, or are about to be used for a licensable activity in order to check that the activity is licensed and/or being conducted in accordance with the premises licence.

- A police officer may enter and search any premises at any time if he has reason to suspect that an offence under the Licensing Act 2003 is being committed or is about to be committed.

- Customs and Excise officers have a right of entry to remove goods liable to forfeiture, e.g. smuggled goods. If entry is demanded at night, the officers must be accompanied by a police officer.

- A police officer or other authorised person may use reasonable force to gain entry in order to exercise the above powers.

13.2. Rights of Entry to Licensed Premises Review Questions

See section 20 for answers

1. Which of the following people do not have right of entry to licensed premises?

(A) A Weights and Measures officer

(B) A Community Support Officer

(C) A fire officer

(D) A building control officer

2. Who has a Right of Entry to Club Premises where there is a Club Premises Certificate in force?

(A) Chief of Police

(B) All police officers

(C) Local residents

(D) Authorised persons having given 48 hours notice

3. In what circumstances do fire officers have right of entry to licensed premises?

(A) At all reasonable times for the purposes of carrying out their statutory duty

(B) At any time of day or night

(C) At any time by appointment

(D) At any time if accompanied by a police offer

4. Who does NOT have a Right of Entry to Licensed Premises where there is a Premises License in force?

(A) Officers of the Security Industry Authority

(B) HM Revenue & Customs

(C) The Licensing Authority or a police officer

(D) The local councillor

14. Illegal Drugs, Smoking and Disorderly Conduct

14.1. Illegal Drug Use

14.1.1. Categories of common illegal drugs

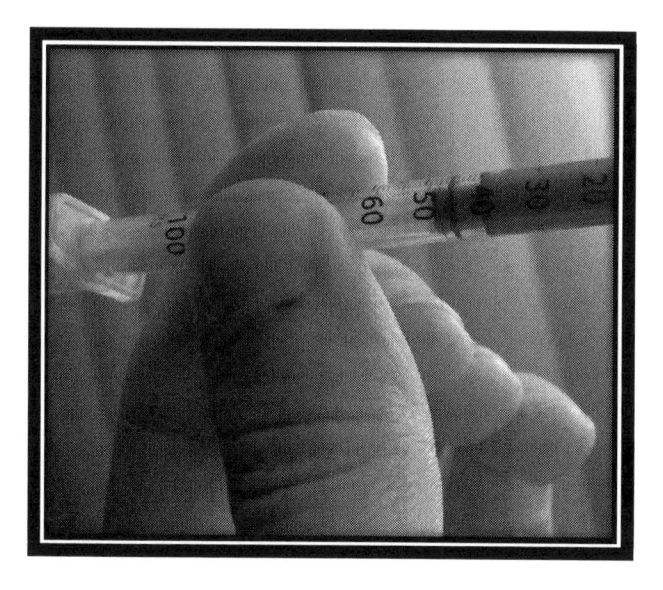

In 1971, the Misuse of Drugs Act was brought into force to regulate the use of 'controlled drugs'.

According to a recent study by the NHS, the number of under 25s admitted to hospital with mental and behavioural problems linked to illegal drug use has risen by 18% in a decade. This figure is approaching 50% in the 25-34 age group.

Class A drugs

So-called 'hard drugs'. The Class A drugs most likely to be encountered on licensed premises are cocaine, 'crack' cocaine, methadone, heroin, acid, MDMA (Ecstasy) and magic mushrooms (penalty - unlimited fine and/or up to 7 years for possession, life for dealing).

Class B drugs

These drugs fall into the middle range in terms of seriousness. The ones most likely to be encountered on licensed premises include amphetamines and cannabis. The herbal drug 'Spice' is similar to cannabis in its effect and became a Class B drug in October 2009 (penalty - unlimited fine and/or up to 5 years for possession, 14 years for dealing).

Class C drugs

Around 40 drugs are listed under this category, 35 of which are tranquillizers. The Class C drugs most likely to be encountered on licensed premises are ketamine, steroids and benzodiazepines, such as mogadon, librium, diazepam and tamgesic. Designer dance drugs such as GBL (Gamma Butyolaclone) and BZP (1-benzylpiperazine) became Class C drugs in October 2009 (unlimited fine and/or up to 2 years for possession, 14 years for dealing).

It is a well known fact that drug dealing takes place in a large percentage of licensed premises. There is a lot at stake for the licence holder with the potential of loss of licence and career should they fail to deal with the problem.

14.1.2. Measures to discourage drug use

- High standards of service and cleanliness are a powerful deterrent to the drugs trade as this shows you care about your venue and look after it and all who use it. Low standards indicate the "don't care" management style dealers will look for. Dealers will not take any unnecessary risks and high proimage management will make them uncomfortable.

- Frequent glass collections, emptying of ashtrays or wiping clean tables provide good excuses for "surveillance".

- Check toilets and other secluded areas regularly for signs of drug use.

- Bar staff are the eyes and ears of the establishment. They need to be alert.

- Consult with the local Licensing Authority to help assess risks of drug-related issues.

14.1.3. Signs of drug use - what to look for

- Pieces of cardboard such as torn up beer mats or cigarette packets left on tables

- Foam stuffing taken from seats or bits of foam left lying around
- Roaches (home made filter tips from cannabis cigarettes)
- Small packets made of folded paper, card or foil.
- Empty sweet wrappings left in toilets.
- Payment with bank notes that have been tightly rolled.
- Traces of powder on toilet seats or other surfaces in toilets
- Very clean surfaces in toilets
- Syringes (caution - these can carry infection so do not touch)
- Spoons or burned tinfoil in toilets

14.1.4. The physical signs of drug use - what to look for

- Very dilated pupils
- Excessive sniffing, dripping nose, watering or red eyes
- Sudden severe cold symptoms following a visit to secluded areas such as the toilet, garden or car park
- White marks or traces of powder round the nose
- Excessive giggling, laughing at nothing, non-stop talking
- Unnaturally dopey, vacant staring, sleepy euphoria
- Non-stop movement, jiggling about
- Excessive consumption of soft drinks
- Sudden inexplicable tearfulness or fright
- Any big alterations in behaviour following trips to secluded areas

14.1.5. Signs of Dealing

- A person who stays for a while but has lots of friends who only stay for short periods
- A person making frequent trips to the toilets, garden or car park followed by different people at the same time
- A person seeming to hide in corners talking very quietly
- Lots of hand or body contact with members of the same sex.
- Dealers are not identifiable by appearance - they may look very respectable.

14. Illegal Drugs, Smoking and Disorderly Conduct

The confiscation or discovery of all drugs must be witnessed and logged in the relevant incident book at the point of seizure. If active drug dealing is identified, the dealer should be kept under observation whilst the police are called.

14.1.6. Penalties for permitting illegal drugs on licensed premises

Heavy penalties can be imposed on those who permit drug related activities to take place on their premises, including supplying and smoking cannabis. This also applies to clubs and temporary events.

14.2. Smoking on Licensed Premises

It is illegal to smoke in any wholly enclosed public place (this includes restaurants, nightclubs, pubs and bars). If you are the person in control of a premises where smoking is allowed to occur, you can be fined up to £2500.

External smoking shelters *may be no more than 50% enclosed* and may require planning consent.

14.3. Disorderly Conduct on Licensed Premises

14.3.1. Allowing disorderly conduct on licensed premise

A person commits the offence of allowing disorderly conduct on licensed premises if they **knowingly allow disorderly conduct** and they have the authority to prevent it. Section 141 of the Licensing Act 2003 does not define what disorderly conduct is but it might include drunkenness, fighting and abusive behaviour.

The categories of person who might commit the offence include:

(a) Any person who works at the premises in a capacity that gives him the authority to sell the alcohol,

(b) A premises licence holder,

(c) A Designated Premises Supervisor,

(d) An officer or member of a club who is present at the time of the sale and who has authority to prevent it, and

(e) A premises user - someone running an event under a Temporary Event Notice.

Any incidents of violent or disorderly behaviour should be logged in a relevant incident book at the time of occurrence.

14.3.2. Sale of alcohol to a person who is drunk

Section 141 of the Licensing Act 2003 also makes it an **offence to sell alcohol to someone who is drunk**, or to allow alcohol to be sold to such a person on relevant premises. The categories of person who may be held responsible for committing the offence are the same as in 14.3.1 above.

14.3.3. Obtaining alcohol for a person who is drunk

It an offence under Section 142 of the Licensing Act 2003 to knowingly **obtain or attempt to obtain** alcohol for consumption on relevant premises **by a person who is drunk**.

14.3.4. Failure to leave licensed premises

Section 143 of the Licensing Act 2003 provides that a **person who is drunk and disorderly commits an offence if he fails to leave** relevant premises at the request of a police constable or of any of the categories of person listed in 14.3.1 above.

14.3.5. Entering or attempting to enter licensed premises

It is also an *offence for a person who is drunk and disorderly to enter or attempt to enter such premises when refused entrance.* A police constable must help to expel drunk or disorderly individuals from relevant premises, or help to prevent them from entering as the case may be, if requested to do so by a licence holder or person in charge of the licensed premises.

14.4. Illegal Drugs, Smoking and Disorderly Conduct Review Questions

See section 20 for answers

1. Who may be charged with serving alcohol to someone who is drunk?

(A) A door supervisor

(B) Anyone authorised to sell alcohol on the premises

(C) Only the DPS

(D) Any member of staff

2. What is the maximum penalty for possession of a Class B substance?

(A) Up to five years' imprisonment and/or fine

(B) A fine only

(C) Imprisonment only

(D) Up to 7 years' imprisonment

3. A personal commits the offence of allowing disorderly conduct on relevant premises if:

(A) They allow disorderly conduct on premises and they do not have the authority to prevent it

(B) The person in authority tries to prevent the disorderly conduct

(C) They knowingly allow disorderly conduct and they have the authority to prevent it

(D) The customer does not help prevent disorderly conduct

4. When assessing the risks to your premises from drug related issues, which of the following groups may best advise you?

(A) Known drug dealers

(B) The Licensing Authority

(C) Staff previously employed

(D) Other local licence holders

5. In what circumstances should drug seizures be recorded in an incident book?

(A) Only when the police are present

(B) Only when found on a member of staff

(C) Only when found on a customer

(D) Whenever drugs are found on the premises

6. What should a licence holder do when a drug dealing activity is identified?

(A) Tell a member of staff to deal with it

(B) Interrupt the activity immediately

(C) Keep the dealer under observation and call the police

(D) Ignore what is happening

15. THE FIRST LICENSING OBJECTIVE: PREVENTION OF CRIME AND DISORDER

In recent years, over half of local authority ***Community Safety Partnerships*** had identified alcohol misuse as a contributory factor to crime. Crime surveys suggest that over 13,000 violent incidents a week take place in or around licensed premises.

Enforcement agencies and licence holders have a duty to do all that is reasonably possible in reducing and preventing crime and disorder in their area. This duty is enabled and enforced by the following legislation:

- Crime and Disorder Act 1998
- Anti-Social Behaviour Act 2003
- Clean Neighbourhoods and Environment Act 2005
- Health Act 2006
- Police and Justice Act 2006
- Violent Crime Reduction Act 2006
- Police and Crime Act 2009
- The Police Reform and Social Responsibility Act 2011

The essential purpose of a licence holder taking responsibility under this objective is to regulate behaviour on their licensed premises. The licence holder can only seek to manage the behaviour of customers inside and within the immediate vicinity of their premises. Beyond that point the licence holder does not have any control.

15.1. Community Safety Partnerships

The 1998 Crime and Disorder Act established Crime and Disorder Reduction Partnerships (now known as Community Safety Partnerships). These local authority partnerships bring together statutory, voluntary and private organisations to help reduce crime in the local area. They are intended to include the licensed retail sector.

It is in the best interests of licence holders to join crime reduction partnerships locally as effective policies for reducing alcohol-related crime and disorder can be implemented.

15.2. Principles of Preventing Crime and Disorder

15.2.1. Know the area

Some pubs are more vulnerable than others to the possibility of violence and disorder. City-centre pubs, estate pubs and male-dominated pubs are more likely to have trouble than country pubs, locals or those that attract a family trade.

15.2.2. Know the customers

A personal licence holder should make a particular point of acknowledging new customers when they walk through the door. It is the friendly thing to do and lets the customer know that they have been noticed. It also subtly begins to establish a climate of control. Personal relationships and the respect that regular customers have for the personal licence holder are critical to exercising sensible control. They will also facilitate the help and co-operation of customers when it is needed.

15.2.3. Early recognition and early intervention

Most violent situations do not just happen without a reason. There is a sequence of events that culminates in an outbreak of violence. A personal licence holder should constantly monitor their customers to detect any potential problems. If a situation begins to escalate early intervention and a friendly word can often prevent it from worsening.

15.2.4. Depersonalise refusal-to-serve encounters

A personal licence holder who refuses service should always try to depersonalise the refusal by making reference to professional and legal obligations. For instance when dealing with a suspected under-age customer, emphasise that it is not a personal matter, but that the personal licence could be at risk if service is provided to an under-age drinker.

15.2.5. Detach troublemakers from groups

Talk to troublemakers away from their friends. Conversely, if the behaviour of a group of people needs to be corrected, talk to them as a group and do not single out individuals in front of their friends. One-to-one communication is more likely to result in co-operation. Having to address an individual in front of friends may lead to a show of aggression.

15.2.6. Give 'face savers'

Focus on the circumstances of an incident rather than the personalities involved.

15.2.7. Provide efficient service

Throughout the session but particularly for 'last orders' - efficiency helps to avoid customers becoming frustrated and aggressive. Regularly clear bottles and glasses from bar and tables - reducing the number of weapons available if conflict does occur.

15.2.8. Responsible drinking

Discourage excessive drinking. Encourage moderate social drinking.

15.2.9. A balanced social mix

Provide family facilities, including food, soft drinks tea and coffee in order to attract a balanced social mix.

15.2.10. Door supervisors

Licence holders must only employ door staff who are registered with the **Security Industry Authority (SIA)**. Door supervisors should be employed:

- During the evening at weekends, on bank holidays and on special occasions, such as festivals and major sporting events
- To monitor and to restrict access to the premises and circulate inside the premises, dealing with troublemakers and escorting them from the premises
- To carry out random drug and weapon searches of customers
- To monitor the flow of customers to prevent overcrowding

15.2.11. Logging information in a crime and disorder *incident book*

Licence holders should keep a book available for staff to record all incidents that happen at the premises and in the immediate vicinity. This record can be used should a crime take place on licensed premises or a complaint is made about the premises or the staff. This record can be used in the licence holder's defence should they attend court or a local authority committee hearing to show due diligence. The defence of due diligence is outlined in section 3.6.4.

The Incident Book should contain the following:

- The date and time of the incident;
- A general description of the incident;
- A description of offenders and or persons involved (with names if possible);
- The member of staff dealing with the incident;
- Any general comments by the staff in relation to possible repercussions etc.

15.3. Voluntary Partnership Schemes

Personal licence holders have a duty to try to minimise crime and disorder in and around licensed premises. This can be greatly facilitated through partnership with the police, other local agencies and the voluntary and community sectors.

Examples of the types of voluntary partnerships that socially responsible licensees can enter into include Best Bar None, Pubwatch, Community Alcohol Partnerships, and Business Improvement Districts.

For instance, the Best Bar None scheme is an awards scheme for all licensed premises across the UK, designed to complement traditional law enforcement by incentivising licensed premises to meet national standards in the way they operate. Such schemes can significantly contribute to their local communities. Since the scheme's 2006 inception in Durham, crimes of violence against the person fell by 58% while footfall increased by 50%. The Government wants to encourage more of these kinds of schemes, which support local growth by reducing crime and disorder.

15.3.1. Benefits of voluntary partnership schemes

Such schemes have a number of positive benefits:
- They help to build a positive and mutually supportive relationship between local personal licence holders and the police
- The police response, when required, is quicker
- Deterrent effect on troublemakers

- Fewer assaults on the person
- Reduced damage to property
- Enhanced trade by the creation of a safer environment
- Licensees and staff feel safer
- Improved public image for the pub

There are times when even well-run premises will have trouble and when the personal licence holder will feel relieved to see the police arrive. Building a positive relationship with the police creates a climate of mutual trust and respect.

15.4. Responsible Drinks Promotions and the Consequences of Irresponsible Promotions

The reason for any drinks promotion needs to be recognised and understood if it is to be managed properly. **Responsible drinks** promotions involve promoting sales in ways that do not contribute to drunkenness or public disorder. Irresponsible drinks promotions that lead to excessive drinking, binge drinking or competitive drinking, undermine the licensing objectives and give licensed retail businesses a bad public image.

The Portman Group, which is the industry responsibility body for drinks producers, offers guidelines about how to offer responsible drinks promotions.

15.4.1. Types of promotions

Licensing authorities have the power to place conditions on a premises licence in respect of drinks promotions. If the use of such powers is to be avoided, licensees need to take seriously the need to adopt a responsible attitude to drinks promotions.

- Promotions carried out in licensed premises generally fall into two main categories:
- Happy Hour promotions (generally price reductions)
- Quantity Incentives (generally buy x drinks for y pounds)

15.4.2. Happy Hours

Happy Hours can be defined as any temporary (i.e. time-limited) discount on a range of drinks that might last for an evening or a shorter period. The concept originated in the United States, and was introduced initially as a way of boosting trade in the traditionally quiet early evening period, by providing alcoholic drinks at lower prices.

Operators need to take a responsible approach to Happy Hours, because customers can sometimes perceive them as encouraging excessive consumption. The following guidelines should be taken into account.

15.4.3. Portman Group guidelines on Happy Hours

Timing - During early evening Happy Hours, some customers may be drinking on an empty stomach, so providing food or bar snacks at these times is helpful.

Duration - Set a clear time period for the promotion. The shorter the Happy Hour and the greater the discount available, the stronger the incentive may be for customers to drink excessively. Happy Hours should last for a sufficient period of time, e.g. two hours, and customers should have information about when Happy Hours start and finish on chalk boards and/or internal notices

Discounts - Take into account that the greater the discount the stronger the incentive may be for some customers to drink excessively. Include soft drinks and low-alcohol or alcohol-free products to ensure customers have an alternative to drinking alcohol cheaply.

Linked discounts - Some practices, for example, discounting drinks according to unpredictable events such as goals or foul play during a football match, would not be a suitable basis for a Happy Hour, and could encourage customers to drink more and to drink more quickly.

15.4.4. Quantity Incentives

Quantity Incentives are any promotions where customers can gain a discount or a prize in exchange for a certain number or quantity of drinks (for consumption on the premises only). Such promotions need to be managed carefully to avoid encouraging excessive consumption.

15.4.5. Portman Group guidelines on Quantity Incentives

Free gifts and other prize incentives - Gifts and other incentives should either be obtainable with the minimum purchase, or should take the form of a proof of purchase collection scheme. Offers requiring the collection of proof of purchase should extend over a suitable period so that there is no encouragement to purchase excessive quantities in a very short timescale

Free drinks - Rewards of free drinks should be offered in the form of vouchers with a reasonable redemption period

Drinking - As a rule, promotions should not involve drinking games which have speed incentives or require large quantities of alcohol to be consumed

Price - Any promotions giving price discounts according to volume purchased need to be proportionate and based on value to the customer

Entry fees - In some circumstances, entry fees entitling customers to reduced price or free drinks on the night, all night, are not appropriate and should be avoided. However, buying a ticket in advance for a function such as a fund-raising dinner-dance is a perfectly acceptable practice.

15.5. Irresponsible Drinks Promotions

A Mandatory Condition of a Premises Licence is that no staff in licensed premises should carry out, arrange or participate in irresponsible drinks promotions. Following the 2012-2013 Alcohol Strategy Consultation the Government intends to increase regulation of drinks promotions. The types of promotions listed below will become irresponsible in all circumstances – removing exemptions and the vagaries of personal judgement.

As discussed previously in Section 8.3, examples of irresponsible drinks promotions are:

- Quantity of alcohol or time-based drinking games
- All you can drink fixed-fee or free alcohol promotions. An exception to this rule has been where the promotion is linked to consumption of a table meal. Following the 2012-2013 Alcohol Strategy Consultation the Government intends to remove this exemption.
- Free or discounted alcohol linked to sporting events (such as free drinks at half-time). Following the 2012-2013 Alcohol Strategy Consultation this specific reference will be removed as the Government believe it to be covered by the regulation of fixed-fee or free alcohol promotions.
- Rewards for consumption of alcohol (T-shirts, event tickets, free alcohol etc.)
- Sales of alcohol linked to promotions which glamorise or condone antisocial behaviour or to refer to the effects of drunkenness in any favourable manner.

There is a separate ban on dispensing alcohol directly into the mouth - e.g. 'Dentist Chair' games. These should not be allowed on the premises even if organised by customers. The only exception is where disability prevents alternative drinking methods. Following the 2012-2013 Alcohol Strategy Consultation this separate condition will be amalgamated into the irresponsible promotion condition.

Finally, the Government has decided to **ban the sale of alcohol at below what it costs the retailer to obtain it in the first place**. This is intended to stop the worst instances of promotional discounting which result in alcohol being sold cheaply and harmfully. It will no longer be legal, for example, to sell a can of 4% ABV lager for less than 40 pence. This measure is scheduled to come into force on the 6th April 2014.

15.6. Penalties Relating to Disorderly Conduct on Licensed Premises

- Allowing disorderly conduct on licensed premises - a fine not exceeding Level 3 on the standard scale (currently *£1,000*).

- Selling alcohol to someone who is drunk - a fine not exceeding Level 3 on the standard scale (currently *£1,000*).

- Knowingly obtaining or attempting to obtain alcohol for someone who is drunk - a fine not exceeding Level 3 on the standard scale (currently *£1,000*).

- Failing to leave licensed premises when requested to do so by an authorised person - a fine not exceeding Level 1 on the standard scale (currently *£200*).

- Entering, or attempting to enter licensed premises when requested no to do so by an authorised person - a fine not exceeding Level 1 on the standard scale (currently *£200*).

15.7. The First Licensing Objective: Prevention of Crime and Disorder Review Questions

See section 20 for answers

1. What is the Best Bar None scheme?

(A) A group of councillors monitoring licensed premises for disorder

(B) A national Awards Scheme for all licensed premises building on Good Practice

(C) The Police Authority checking personal licence holders for criminal convictions

(D) A group of people advertising special events in licensed premises

2. Which of the following is a licensing objective?

(A) The prevention of crime and disorder

(B) To promote more liberal licensing hours

(C) More healthy drinking habits by customers

(D) A more responsible approach by licensees towards customer service

3. How can individuals become involved in Community Safety Partnerships

(A) By contacting the Licensing Authority's community safety section or local police licensing officer

(B) By obtaining a personal licence

(C) By contributing to local charitable events

(D) By owning a Licensed Premises

4. What specific meetings can personal licence and premises licence holders attend to discuss local licensing issues and emerging problems?

(A) Pass meetings

(B) Carlsberg breweries meetings

(C) Pubwatch or Retail Watch meetings

(D) Burgermaster meetings

5. Why should individuals involved in the Licensed trade become involved in a Pubwatch/Retail Watch scheme?

(A) To satisfy the Licensing Authority that a Personal License should be renewed

(B) To detect and prevent crime in conjunction with the local police

(C) To socialise with other license holders

(D) To encourage competition amongst licensed premises

16. THE SECOND LICENSING OBJECTIVE: PUBLIC SAFETY

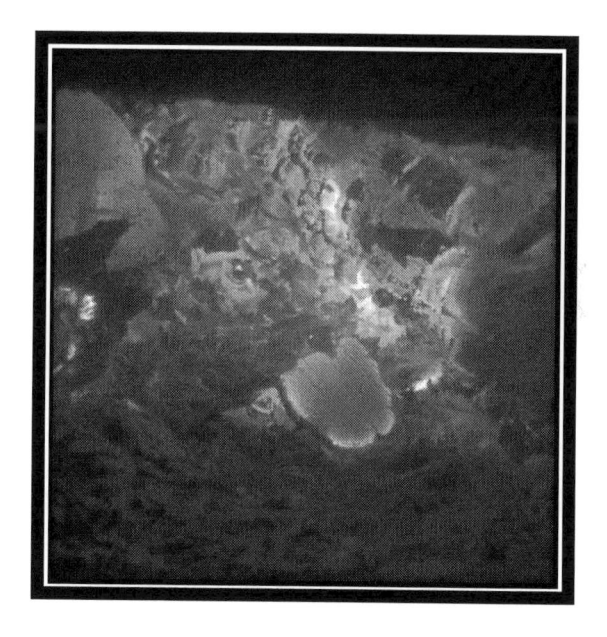

Complying with the Licensing Objective to ensure Public Safety is paramount in obtaining a premises licence to sell or supply alcohol. Applicants must be able to demonstrate an awareness and compliance with health and safety, and fire prevention legislation.

The British Beer and Pub Associations (BBPA) has published its own industry guidance which can be found on its website: http://www.beerandpub.com

16.1. The Regulatory Reform (Fire Safety) Order 2005 - Fire Risk Assessment

The Regulatory Reform (Fire Safety) Order 2005 came into effect in October 2006 and replaced over 70 pieces of fire safety law. The requirement for businesses to have fire certificates has been abolished.

Under this Order, the responsible person (the employer or person in charge of the business) must carry out a fire safety risk assessment and implement and maintain a fire management plan. The law emphasises preventing fires and reducing risk and makes it the responsibility of the premises holder to ensure the safety of everyone who uses the premises, or is within the immediate vicinity.

More detailed advice and guidance on the implementation of a fire risk management plan can be found on the GOV.UK website (https://www.gov.uk/workplace-fire-safety-your-responsibilities).

16.2. Control of Noise at Work Regulations 2005 - Noise Risk Assessments

The Control of Noise at Work Regulations 2005 has been in effect for the music and entertainment sector since 6 April 2008. The music and entertainment sector is defined in the Noise Regulations as "all workplaces where (a) live music is played; or (b) recorded music is played in a restaurant, bar, public house, discotheque or nightclub, or alongside live music or a live dramatic or dance performance."

The Regulations set lower exposure limits than those currently applied under the 1989 Regulations and place certain duties on employers to:

- Assess the risk to employees of noise at work
- Take action to reduce noise exposure
- Provide employees with hearing protection (only where the noise cannot be reduced)
- Provide instruction and training to employees
- Carry out health surveillance (where there is a risk to health)

More detailed advice and guidance can be found on the BBPA's website (http://www.beerandpub.com). Nevertheless, all premises, especially those playing amplified music at noise levels above 80db, are encouraged to undertake a risk assessment and identify how staff exposure can be reduced.

16.3. Other Public Safety Measures

Care should be taken to ensure that other, obvious public safety risks are taken into account:

- **Free drinking water** should be available at all times where reasonably available (particularly in dance venues due to the likelihood of overheating). *This is now a mandatory condition* for all premises licences.

- The air management system within the premises must have sufficient capacity for the volume of premises it services.

- Special effects such as strobe lighting, smoke, foam, lasers, pyrotechnics, dry ice or bubbles should not be used unless full safety controls are put in place.

- There should be adequate first aid arrangements at all times.

- Gangways, exit routes and steps should be maintained in good order with non-slippery and even surfaces, edges of steps and stairways should be well marked.

- Barriers will be provided to control queuing patrons to prevent crushing.

- Sufficient numbers of staff who are suitably trained in emergency procedures should be provided on the premises, depending on the activities or entertainment

- Where glazing forms part of windows, walls or partitions below waist height it should be constructed of safety materials. Where glazing forms part of a door or side panel at below shoulder height it will also be constructed of safety materials.

- Regular glass and bottle collection should be undertaken throughout opening hours.

- The provision of plastic glasses and bottles should be reviewed depending on the type of entertainment provided and the number and behaviour of patrons attending. Plastic glasses should be provided for outside drinking areas.

- A means of addressing patrons during operating hours, which can be heard above entertainment, or a means of interrupting the entertainment to make important safety announcements should be available.

16.4. The New 'Health-Related' Objective

The Police Reform and Social Responsibility Act 2011 added Primary Care Trusts in England and Local Health Boards (LHBs) in Wales to the list of responsible authorities under the Licensing Act 2003. They now have input into local decisions about alcohol licensing with the overall goal of improving public health.

Whilst stopping short of creating a fifth licensing objective, the Police Reform and Social Responsibility Act 2011 provides a additional 'health-related' objective *for use in circumstances where alcohol-related health issues are a concern*. For example, if a high incidence of alcohol-related hospital admissions are linked to a specific premises, the relevant health body can now apply for a licence review. Such a disorderly premises would however be normally expected to come to the attention of the police under the original terms of the Licensing Act 2003 prior to this becoming necessary.

Of potentially greater relevance is the application of the additional health objective in areas with a high density of licensed premises such as *Cumulative Impact Areas* (see section 5.7). As alcohol-related health issues can be significant in such busy, often city-centre, areas, the new Act will allow health bodies to object to the granting of new licences. The health body will consequently need to be notified of new premises licence applications.

When making a representation, ***the health body will need to be able to collect anonymised information*** about incidents relating to specific premises or premises in cumulative impact areas. Examples of such information could include anonymised data on A&E attendances, ambulance journeys and hospital admissions following alcohol-related accidents, fights, glassings, other injuries and alcohol poisoning.

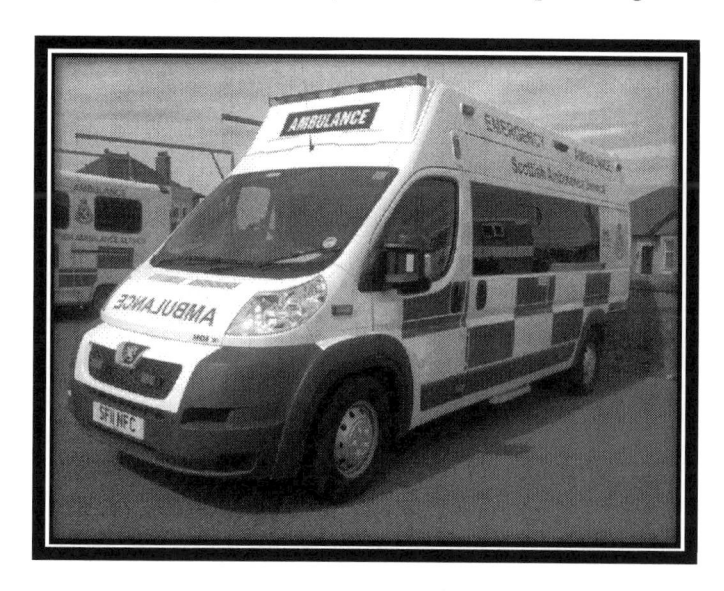

It should be noted that Primary Care Trusts were abolished on the 31st March 2013 following changes introduced in the Health and Social Care Act 2012. The role of responsible authority is now fulfilled by the Director of Public Health in each (upper tier or unitary) local authority area.

16.5. The Second Licensing Objective: Public Safety Review Questions

See section 20 for answers

1. What is the principle mechanism for enforcing fire safety on licensed premises?

(A) The Regulatory Reform (Fire Safety) Order 2005

(B) The Fire Certificate

(C) The Licensing Act 2003

(D) Health and Safety at Work etc Act 1974

2. What must a person responsible for a licensed premises do to ensure fire safety?

(A) Carry out a fire safety risk assessment only

(B) Maintain a fire management plan only

(C) Carry out a risk assessment and maintain a fire management plan

(D) Consult with the local fire service

3. The Control of Noise at Work Regulations 2005 governs which types of workplaces?

(A) Pubs or clubs undergoing renovation with ongoing construction work only

(B) Concert venues playing live music only

(C) Venues playing live music or recorded music played in a restaurant, bar, public house, discotheque or nightclub

(D) Venues with live performances only

17. THE THIRD LICENSING OBJECTIVE - PREVENTION OF PUBLIC NUISANCE

17.1. How is Public Nuisance defined?

Preventing public nuisance is one of the four licensing objectives and like the other three it must be regarded as an aspiration. It is clearly not possible for any premises owner to guarantee that nothing happening in or around the premises will ever annoy a member of the public.

Public nuisance is not defined narrowly within the context of the Licensing Act 2003 and Licensing Authorities are likely to take a broad approach to its meaning.

In effect, a public nuisance may be classified as ***any nuisance arising from a licensable activity***. This may range from major noise pollution from an outdoor pop concert affecting a wide area, to a low level nuisance affecting only a few people. For example, vibrations from a poorly mounted extraction duct serving a pub kitchen could be included in the definition of public nuisance. The release of unpleasant smells may also be considered a nuisance.

The concept of public nuisance doesn't cover everything that may annoy the public but if the impact of licensed activities is disproportionate, or markedly reduces the amenity value of the area to local people, the local Licensing Authorities will take account of this when exercising their licensing functions. What this may mean in practice is that, if other legislation proves inadequate for control purposes, the Licensing Authority may consider imposing restrictive licensing conditions in the premises licence.

It is therefore in the licence holder's interests to **carry out a risk assessment** prior to the launch of new entertainment to check that a public nuisance is not created.

Those operating premises with a premises licence need to be sensitive to the impact that their activities may have on people who have to live, work and sleep within the local vicinity of a licensed premises.

Environmental Health Officers (EHO), as well as the police, now have the power to close a licensed premises on the grounds of public nuisance. The new power derives from the Anti-Social Behaviour Act 2003.

17.2. Penalties for Breach of Public Nuisance

Forfeiture of personal licence or suspension of licence for up to six months with a fine of 1-5 on the standard scale.

17.3. The Third Licensing Objective: Prevention of Public Nuisance Review Questions

See section 20 for answers

1. What does 'EHO' stand for?

(A) Electrical Health Officer

(B) Early Hour Order

(C) Exemplary Hygiene Officer

(D) Environmental Health Officer

2. When should a Noise Assessment be carried out?

(A) During a performance

(B) Prior to launching new entertainment

(C) During performance rehearsals

(D) When the venue is closed

3. How is a local authority most likely to deal with noisy premises or events?

(A) Pass it on to the police

(B) By using the Health and Safety at Work Act

(C) Under the Anti-Social Behaviour Act

(D) Contact the Noise Abatement Society

4. What could be the penalty for committing a noise and vibration nuisance affecting a few people living locally?

(A) Forfeiture of your personal licence or suspension of your licence for up to 6 months

(B) There is no penalty for committing a noise and vibration nuisance

(C) Forfeiture of your personal licence or suspension of your licence for up to 6 months together with a fine ranging from level 1-5 on the standard scale

(D) A fine ranging from level 1-5 on the standard scale

5. What can help assess if there are noise level problems?

(A) Sound level meters

(B) Excessive beer consumption on the premises

(C) A trained dog

(D) Asking the Designated Premises Supervisor

18. THE FOURTH LICENSING OBJECTIVE: PROTECTION OF CHILDREN

The Licensing Act 2003 defines a *"child"* as *a person of less than 16 years of age*. Protection of children is one of the four licensing objectives and the Act details a number of offences designed to protect children in licensed premises. The objective is to ensure that licensed premises offer a safe environment for children in terms of their physical, moral and psychological welfare. Children should be unable to access alcohol or drugs, and be subject to an appropriate level of care and supervision at all times.

18.1. Sale of Alcohol to Young Persons

Existing legislation ties the offence of selling alcohol to under-age children to licensed premises. Under Section 146 of the Licensing Act 2003 *it is an offence to sell alcohol to a person under the age of 18.*

18. The Fourth Licensing Objective: Protection of Children

Under Section 147 of the Licensing Act 2003, **it is an offence to <u>allow</u> the sale of alcohol to a person under the age of 18**. This offence may be committed by any person who works on the premises in a capacity that gives them the authority to prevent the sale or, in the case of a club, the supply of alcohol to a child under 18.

18.2. Sale of Liqueur Confectionery to Children

Under Section 148 of the Licensing Act 2003 (as initially drafted) it was an offence to sell or supply liqueur confectionery to a child under the age of 16. **This offence was repeale**d by the Deregulation Act 2015 on 26 May 2015 and need no longer be considered.

18.3. Defences to the Above Offences – The Age Verification Policy

The defence for the person who physically made the sale i.e. a member of staff is that **all reasonable steps were taken** to avoid commission of the offence:

1. The young person was asked for evidence of their age and that the evidence produced was of a kind that would have convinced any reasonable person, or

2. That nobody could reasonably have suspected from the young person's appearance that they were under 18.

The defence for anyone else charged in connection with a sale (e.g. the employer of the member of staff who made the sale, or one of the personal licence holders) is that they exercised all due diligence to avoid the commission of the offence. **Due diligence** means setting up a system to prevent offences being committed, and monitoring that system to ensure that it is effective and that staff are following it. Clear policies and effective staff training are essential to showing a due diligence defence.

Note that it is now a **mandatory licence condition** for all premises selling alcohol to have an **age verification policy** requiring staff to check the ID of anyone who appears to be under 18 years of age (or any such older age as may be specified in the policy). Note that following the 2012-2013 Alcohol Strategy Consultation the Government has made it clear that the responsibility for implementing an age verification policy lies with the Designated Premises Supervisor, already responsible for the day-to-day management of the premises.

The Violent Crime Reduction Act 2006 introduced the new offence of ***persistently selling alcohol to children***. Under these changed provisions any person found guilty of selling alcohol to children ***2 times in 3 consecutive months*** faces ***an unlimited fine*** and possible licence suspension. There is no due diligence defence for this.

18.4. The Proof of Age Standards Scheme

As a basic minimum, a premises must have a policy that requires people who appear to be under the age of 18 to be asked, before being served alcohol, to produce identification showing their:

- Photograph
- Date of birth
- A holographic mark.

NB: Following the 2012-2013 Alcohol Strategy Consultation the Government intends to also allow age-verification documents bearing ultra-violet fluorescent ink as some foreign passports and identity cards do not bear the necessary holographic mark.

In accordance with these requirements, photo driving licences or passports are valid proofs of age. However, in the absence of a national identity card the Proof of Age Standards Scheme (***PASS***) acts as a national guarantee scheme for proof-of-age cards. The scheme was launched to bring in a common, recognisable standard with a robust accreditation process. Examples of national suppliers of PASS photo-ID cards are CitizenCard, ProofGB, Validate UK and Young Scot. The ***PASS hologram*** included on each card indicates that the card issuer has passed a rigorous audit process carried out by Trading Standards Officers.

In the year 2000 there were 283 licensed retailers successfully prosecuted or cautioned for selling alcohol to under-18s. The need for the PASS scheme, launched in 2003, was hence very clear.

18.4.1. Application for a PASS accredited card

The requirements of card suppliers do vary, however an applicant is likely to be asked to provide one or more of the following:

- Copy of applicant's Birth Certificate. The applicant may be asked to get this verified by a referee who has seen the original.
- Copy of the back page of the applicant's passport which details personal information and a photograph

- Sample of the applicant's signature
- Copy of a photo driving licence
- Copy of the applicant's medical card

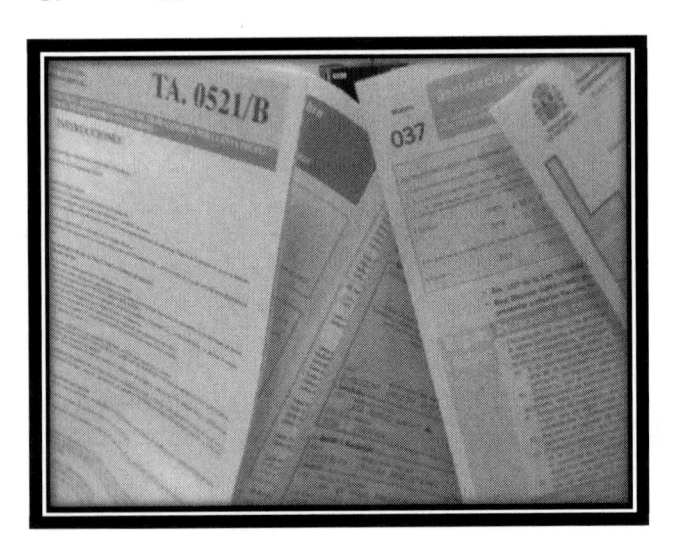

18.5. Prohibition of Unsupervised Sales by Children

It is an *offence* for a responsible person knowingly *to allow an individual under the age of 18* to sell or, in the case of a club, to supply alcohol *unless each sale or supply has been specifically approved by a responsible person*. A young person under 18 serving alcohol in a bar, where each sale or supply is specifically approved by the licensee, is in practice likely to mean a young person on a Modern Apprenticeship scheme.

Exception: Alcohol sales in dining areas - no offence is committed if the alcohol is sold for consumption with a table meal in a part of the premises used only for this purpose. The effect of this exception is that, for example, a minor will be able to serve alcohol in a restaurant or in the dedicated dining area of a pub.

18.6. Purchase of Alcohol by Young Persons

Section 149 of the Licensing Act 2003 makes it *an offence for a child under 18 to buy or attempt to buy alcohol* whether or not on licensed premises, or, if he is a member of a club, for him to have alcohol supplied to him by the club.

18.7. Test Purchasing

A purchase or attempted purchase, *of alcohol by a child under 18 will not be an offence if the child was asked to do so by a police constable, weights and measures inspector or trading standards officer.* This applies so long as these authorities are acting in the course of their duty to conduct test purchasing operations to establish whether licensees and staff working in licensed premises are complying with the prohibition on underage sales.

18.8. Consumption of Alcohol by Young Persons

Under Section 150 of the Licensing Act 2003 *it is an offence for a person under the age of 18 to knowingly consume alcohol on relevant premises.* The offence is thus not be committed if the child inadvertently consumes the alcohol, for example if their drink is spiked. In addition, *16 and 17 year olds can drink beer, wine or cider with a table meal* so long as they are accompanied by an adult who purchases the alcohol.

It is also an *offence for an authorised person to knowingly allow the consumption of alcohol by a person under 18 on relevant premises.* The categories of person who may commit the offence are the same as for the other offences.

18.9. Delivering Alcohol to Children

Section 151 of the Act sets out offences relating to the delivery of alcohol, to children. *It is an offence for someone working on relevant premises knowingly to deliver to a child alcohol* that is sold on the premises or supplied there on behalf of a club. The offence would cover, for example circumstances where a child takes delivery of a consignment of alcohol bought by his father from an off-licence.

Exceptions:

Delivery to home or place of work - an offence is not committed if the alcohol is delivered to the home or place of work of the purchaser (for example, where a child opens the door and signs for the delivery of his father's order at his house).

When the minor was doing his job - an offence is not committed where the job of the minor who took delivery involves delivery of alcohol (for example, where a 16 year old office worker is sent to collect a delivery for his employer), nor where the alcohol is sold or supplied for consumption on the relevant premises.

18.10. Sending a Child to Obtain Alcohol

Section 152 of the Act makes it an ***offence to knowingly send a child to obtain alcohol*** that is sold or supplied for consumption off the premises. The offence would cover, for example, circumstances where a parent sends their child to an off-licence to collect alcohol that had been bought over the telephone. The same exceptions apply as for the offences above.

18.11. Allowing Children on to Licensed Premises

It is ***unlawful*** under Section 145 of the Licensing Act 2003 ***to allow unaccompanied children aged less than 16 years into:***

- Licensed premises where alcohol is supplied mostly for consumption on the premises
- Licensed premises which do not rely solely upon the sale of alcohol (e.g. restaurants) between the hours of 12am and 5am

18.12. Penalties for Breach

- A purchase or attempted purchase of alcohol by someone under 18: a fine not exceeding **Level 3 on the standard scale**. In the case of an offence committed by a person acting as an agent for a child under the age of 18 - **an unlimited fine** (see s85 of the Legal Aid, Sentencing and Punishment of Offenders Act 2012).

- Knowingly allowing the consumption of alcohol by someone under 18 - a fine not exceeding Level 3 on the standard scale (for an under 18 committing the offence). An unlimited fine for all other cases.

- Delivering alcohol sold or supplied on relevant premises to under 18: an unlimited fine.

- Sending an under 18 to obtain alcohol sold or supplied on relevant premises for consumption off the premises: an unlimited fine.

- Allowing on relevant premises an under 18 to sell or supply alcohol: : an unlimited fine.

NB: Standard scale of Fines at time of going to press:

Level	-	Maximum Fine
1	-	£200
2	-	£500
3	-	£1,000
4	-	£2,500
5	-	£5,000 - from 12 March 2015 (non-retrospective application): an **unlimited fine** on summary conviction.

18.13. The Fourth Licensing Objective: Protection of Children Review Questions

See section 20 for answers

1. What is the definition of a 'child' under the Licensing Act 2003?

(A) Someone under the age of 21

(B) Someone under the age of 16

(C) Someone under the age of 18

(D) Someone with a mental age of 16 who is in fact older

2. At what times is it unlawful to allow unaccompanied children into premises where alcohol is supplied?

(A) Between 7pm to 6am

(B) Between 9pm to 5am

(C) Between 12am to 5am

(D) Between 7pm to 1am

3. Which of the following is the best established proof of age scheme?

(A) Connexions card

(B) Citizen Card

(C) Validate UK

(D) PASS card with hologram

4. Which of the following would not be committing an offence?

(A) Knowingly delivering alcohol to a minor on behalf of relevant premises

(B) Delivering an order of alcohol to a purchaser's home and a minor signing for it

(C) Knowingly supplying alcohol to a minor in qualifying club

(D) Knowingly selling alcohol to a minor in an off licence

5. At what age is it permitted to enter a licensed premises selling alcohol unaccompanied?

(A) 16 years of age

(B) 12 years of age

(C) 14 years of age

(D) There is no age limit

6. Premises used mainly or solely for consumption of alcohol may only admit children under 16 years of age:

(A) Before 9pm

(B) Before lunchtime

(C) When accompanied by an adult

(D) On weekends except during school holidays

19. Hearings and Appeals

19.1. Licensing Committees

The purpose of the licensing committee is to discharge the licensing functions of Licensing Authorities, including hearing applications and appeals but not including the publication of the licensing statement.

Each Licensing Authority must establish a licensing committee of **between 10 and 15 members**.

19.2. The Purpose and Procedures of Licensing Hearings

The basic purpose of licensing hearings is the determination of applications for personal licences, premises licences and club certificates, Temporary Event Notices and variations to premises licences or applications for the revocation of personal and premises licences.

If there are valid representations (objections to the grant of the license) received within the consultation period then a **hearing must be convened** in order that the licensing committee of the Licensing Authority can determine the outcome of the application. However, if all parties involved in the application process agree that a hearing is not necessary then an informally negotiated decision may be reached.

The procedures of licensing hearings are delegated by the Licensing Authority to its licensing committee. A licensing committee may establish one or more sub-committees consisting of **three members of the main committee**.

19.3. Delegation of Functions

The full committee, or a sub-committee, may delegate its functions to an officer of the committee. However, officers of the committee may not deal with matters in respect of which representations or objections have been made, and with which it is appropriate for the licensing committee or one of its sub-committees to deal.

19.4. Licensing Hearings

19.4.1. The hearing process

The chairman is in charge of the proceedings. The following sequence of events is for guidance but individual hearings may differ:

- The chairman explains the format for the meeting and asks everyone to introduce themselves
- The licensing officer outlines the application
- The applicant (or their representative) speaks in support of their application and calls witnesses
- Objectors ask the applicant (or their representative) and witnesses questions
- Members of the panel ask the applicant (or their representative) and witnesses questions Objectors speak about their representation and call any witnesses
- The applicant (or their representative) asks the objectors questions
- Members of the panel ask questions
- The chairman asks everyone if they want to add anything further

- The chairman asks everyone to leave the room while the panel reaches a decision - the council's lawyer and committee note-taker remain

- Once a decision has been made, everyone is invited to come back in to hear it, although for complex applications, the panel may decide to give its decision later.

Representation of Parties: Any party may be represented by another whether they are legally qualified or not. In cases of multiple objections from members of the public the licensing committee recommends the appointment of a single spokesperson for the group who will coordinate questions and comments for the group.

Legal Advice: Any legal advice will be either given in open session or repeated to everyone present.

Witnesses: Any party wishing to call a witness to give evidence must request permission to do so in advance of the hearing. Notice must be given of the name of the witness and the points they will deal with in evidence. Notice must usually be received by the Council at least 5 days before the hearing. No party has an automatic right to cross examine a witness and must seek permission from the Chairman of the licensing committee to do so.

Exclusion of the Public: *Hearings will usually be in public.* However, the licensing committee may exclude the public (including a part to the hearing) if it is in the public interest to do so.

Adjournments: The licensing committee may adjourn proceedings where appropriate but only for good reason. The licensing committee may however proceed in any parties absence in the interest of justice.

19.4.2. The decision

The licensing committee may grant the licence as applied for, refuse to grant the licence, grant the licence in a modified state, e.g. shorter hours, or with added conditions, exclude a licensable activity from the licence or refuse to specify a given person as the DPS. The licensing committee will usually invite comment upon proposed conditions before imposing them and will only decide to impose conditions where it is necessary to refuse the application before them.

19.5. The Licensing Appeal Procedure

The purpose of the appeals procedure is to provide for a **system of appeals to the magistrates' court** against the decisions of the Licensing Authority. Any party involved in that decision may appeal against it, i.e. applicants, responsible authorities or interested parties.

The grounds for any appeal must focus on the four licensing objectives:

1. *The prevention of crime and disorder*
2. *Public safety (including the additional Health Objective)*
3. *The prevention of public nuisance*
4. *The protection of children from harm*

For example, an applicant for a premises licence may appeal to a magistrates' court against the inclusion in the licence by the Licensing Authority of conditions that the applicant sees as unreasonably restrictive. At the same time, the police or a local resident would have a right of appeal against conditions that appeared to them to fail to promote the licensing objectives.

19.6. Hearings and Appeals Review Questions

See section 20 for answers

1. Who can appeal against a decision by a Licensing Authority?

(A) Any person who has made relevant representations during the course of the application

(B) Any person who lives locally

(C) Anyone in business locally

(D) The Magistrates' Court

2. A hearing of a police notice of objection to a temporary event may be avoided

(A) Where the police and the organiser agree to modify the application

(B) When there is no time for a hearing before the event is due

(C) Where the applicant decides to use another venue

(D) Only where the application is withdrawn

3. Which one of the following hears an appeal against the decision of a Licensing Authority?

(A) Crown Court

(B) Magistrates' Court

(C) Secretary of State

(D) Chief Officer of Police

4. A Licensing Authority sub-committee must consist of 3 persons, who are selected from

(A) The local council

(B) The local magistrates

(C) The main licensing committee body

(D) The local police

19. Hearings and Appeals

5. How many members does the Licensing Committee have?

(A) 5

(B) 10

(C) 15

(D) Between 10 and 15

20. QUIZ ANSWERS

Section	Answers
3: Licensable Activities	Q1: B, Q2: B, Q3: A, Q4: A, Q5: D
4: Alcohol in a Nutshell	Q1: B, Q2: A, Q3: C, Q4: C. Q5: C, Q6: D
5: Licensing Authorities	Q1: C, Q2: D, Q3: B, Q4: B
6: Personal Licence	Q1: A, Q2: B, Q3: D, Q4: B, Q5: B
7: Duties of the Personal Licence holder	Q1: D, Q2: D, Q3: B, Q4: B
8: Premises Licence	Q1: B, Q2: C, Q3: B, Q4: D, Q5: B, Q6: D
9: Clubs	Q1: A, Q2: C, Q3: A, Q4: C, Q5: A, Q6: B
10: Permitted Temporary Activities	Q1: C, Q2: D, Q3: A, Q4: D, Q5: A
11: Suspension and Closure – the police	Q1: D, Q2: C, Q3: C, Q4: A, Q5: B, Q6: C
12: Closure Powers – the Local Authority	Q1: B, Q2: C, Q3: B, Q4: C, Q5: C
13: Rights of Entry to Licensed Premises	Q1: B, Q2: D, Q3: A, Q4: D
14: Illegal Drugs and Disorderly Conduct on Licensed Premises	Q1: B, Q2: A, Q3: C, Q4: B, Q5: D, Q6: C
15: The First Licensing Objective – Prevention of Crime and Disorder	Q1: B, Q2: A, Q3: A, Q4: C, Q5: B
16: The Second Licensing Objective – Public Safety	Q1: A, Q2: C, Q3: C
17: The Third Licensing Objective – Prevention of Public Nuisance	Q1: D, Q2: B, Q3: C, Q4: C, Q5: A
18: The Fourth Licensing Objective – Protection of Children from Harm	Q1: B, Q2: C, Q3: D, Q4: B, Q5: A, Q6: C
19: Hearings and Appeals	Q1: A, Q2: A, Q3: B, Q4: C, Q5: D

Printed in Great Britain
by Amazon